T0289785

ROUTLEDGE LIBRARY EDITIONS:
THE ECONOMICS AND BUSINESS OF
TECHNOLOGY

Volume 13

COMPUTERS, MANAGEMENT AND INFORMATION

COMPUTERS, MANAGEMENT AND INFORMATION

DAVID FIRNBERG

Routledge
Taylor & Francis Group

LONDON AND NEW YORK

First published in 1973 by George Allen & Unwin

This edition first published in 2018
by Routledge
2 Park Square, Milton Park, Abingdon, Oxon OX14 4RN

and by Routledge
711 Third Avenue, New York, NY 10017

Routledge is an imprint of the Taylor & Francis Group, an informa business

© 1973 George Allen & Unwin Ltd

British Library Cataloguing in Publication Data
A catalogue record for this book is available from the British Library

ISBN: 978-1-138-50336-6 (Set)
ISBN: 978-1-351-06690-7 (Set) (ebk)
ISBN: 978-0-8153-6826-7 (Volume 13) (hbk)
ISBN: 978-1-351-25536-3 (Volume 13) (ebk)

Publisher's Note
The publisher has gone to great lengths to ensure the quality of this reprint but points out that some imperfections in the original copies may be apparent.

Disclaimer
The publisher has made every effort to trace copyright holders and would welcome correspondence from those they have been unable to trace.

COMPUTERS MANAGEMENT AND INFORMATION

DAVID FIRNBERG

London

GEORGE ALLEN AND UNWIN LTD

RUSKIN HOUSE   MUSEUM STREET

First published in 1973

© George Allen & Unwin Ltd 1973

ISBN 0 04 658142 1

Printed in Great Britain
in 11 point Times Roman
by The Aldine Press, Letchworth, Herts

Contents

Plates

Introduction

A gulf still exists between people and computers; between those who make the computers work: the technicians, the programmers, the systems analysts; and those whom the computers should serve: the managers, the clerks, the civil servants, the public.

This book tries to bridge the gulf. Its purpose is to dispel the mystique surrounding computers by demonstrating that it is not only necessary for the manager to control the computer and make it serve him, but also possible!

Computers are now progressing beyond the stage of being regarded merely as gigantic calculating machines only able to fulfil the straightforward day-to-day operations of processing data; handling payrolls, invoices and stock control; and maintaining records for building societies, banks, N.H.I., income tax, motor licences, libraries and so forth. Their ability to undertake such routine tasks at speed is generally well recognized as are also their occasional impersonal inaccuracies. This book looks at the next stage: the use of the computer to help to organize human activity. In particular it explores the ways in which those in command—the managers—can use computers to provide them with information which will help them do their job and make their decisions.

Every decision is taken by a person or group of people. A decision is made to initiate action or change the course of action already under way. A management decision must be defined as one that cannot be taken on purely quantitative, logical grounds; if it could it would not represent management action, but merely automatic or routine action. The computer cannot exercise judgement but it can follow a set of rules; judgement must be exercised in setting these rules, but once established, the computer can be relied upon to follow them absolutely.

People are therefore the essential ingredient in the making of management decisions: people who absorb information deriving from the formal reporting structures of the organization, from informal information gleaned by personal observation, from informed contacts with other people, from their own individual experience. All of these sources of information contribute to the exercise of intuition and judgement which results in a decision being made.

Computers can only contribute one thing to this process of decision-making: they supply a resource of computing power in the same way that an electricity generating station provides a resource of electricity. This is an important point; the parallel with electricity is quite apt. In the early days of electricity a manager would quite probably have said, 'What I need to do my job is an electricity generator.' Nowadays all he says he needs is access to an outlet of electricity; indeed he can usually take it for granted that such access will be readily available. In the same pattern, since computers are still in their early days, managers are still saying, 'What I need in order to do my job is a computer', when the most they really require is access to computing power.

Computers are costly: not only the hardware, but also the software, the programming, the systems design, the education, the failures. This book suggests that, besides reviewing the contribution which computers can make to management and information, it is necessary to consider the initiative which management must assume in order to optimize this contribution.

Also the book will explore various systems which can be designed for using computing power to assist those responsible for decision making. It is intended to demonstrate that the full potential of computing power is not likely to be exploited unless the organization develops a corporate policy on a number of activities directly affected by this power. With such a policy the power of computing will allow the organization to do many things that could not be done before, thereby improving the quality of the decisions made and their responsiveness to current and future situations.

The computer provides the opportunity for tackling old problems in a new way, but too many computer systems are developed out of theory derived from a comprehensive study of the existing situation. A survey is undertaken to establish the 'information requirements' of the managers and of the system they operate. A three-year project is launched to develop for them the perfect system which will provide all their requirements. In due time the analysts present and introduce their system into the operation, only to find that it does not work, it does not provide the information the managers now require, and it is met with a barrage of abuse as being yet another of those fancy theoretical systems. 'Ah, yes,' say the analysts, 'but this is what you asked for—look, here is your signature on the project definition!'

Maybe it is what they asked for, but they asked for it three years ago, when what they required reflected the circumstances in which they were then operating and the depth of their own understanding of their job. If they had had that system three years ago, they would have welcomed it—for a while. Little by little, however, new things would be required, modifications; by using the system the manager would have come to learn more about his job and so have a better understanding of the information he really needed to control his operation. Perhaps the Government has since introduced a new tax, or the competitor a new product. The manager, cap in hand, then goes to his computer people and says, 'I know I said I wanted a system looking like this, but what I really want is . . .' The D.P. Manager throws up his hands in horror and replies, 'But that means six months' re-programming!'

As time passes the organization becomes disillusioned with its computer activity; it finds it difficult to pinpoint what is wrong: although the D.P. unit has an insatiable appetite for computer time, and produces a volume of print-out, its impact on the actual operation is decreasing steadily. At the same time it is imposing an increasing burden upon the organization; its inexorable logic demands vast data-checking operations, but its output contributes little. Old manual systems are given a new lease of life because of the management frustration— entrepreneurial managements have a heyday of demonstrating their ability to manage and to react to new situations far better than those conscientiously trying to use the computer.

It is often easier to examine the means than to determine the ends, but when the means are perfected they are found to be quite irrelevant to the end. This can be the case in inexperienced model building where the modellers say, 'If only I had more data . . .' Significant effort is then mounted to collect the data, often 'once only' data, only to find it is irrelevant to the real needs of the model once the problem has been further explored. Models do not initially need masses of data, only an understanding of the problem; models permit an exploration of the significant operating relationships; further modelling isolates the degree of accuracy needed in the data. Only then should the data requirements be established. To be useful a model must be alive, it must progress, it must reflect the up-to-date situation. Thus, updated data is essential, but only in a limited quantity and to an established degree of accuracy. One wonders how many cobwebbed files of 'once only' data exist, collected at great expense and then never really used.

These problems result from one situation: the computer is here to serve, but the organization or community it is serving is constantly experiencing change, so the computer's contribution must change accordingly.

The understanding of what the computer can do and how it can be used to react to the dynamics of society must lie with society itself, not merely with its technicians. The needs of society, of organizations, are not technical needs; they are down-to-earth common-sense needs and it is up to the managers to express those needs and insist

13

that they are met. This book strives to assist managers to do just that.

The author has many people to thank, too many to name individually. Experience comes from doing, but it also comes from absorbing other people's ideas, and this book presents an amalgam of practice and ideas. Most of all the ideas have been generated by highly professional colleagues with whom the author has been working for some years in developing and introducing an Integrated Management Information System into ICL, the largest manufacturer of computers in the world outside the United States.

The author would particularly like to acknowledge the support he has received from ICL, and to express his gratitude to them for allowing him to draw so heavily upon his experience with them.

Chapter 1

Science and Society

The beginning

The brain likes to give a label; it likes to categorize, to identify, to group. Each experience, each new event or encounter is compartmentalized. Once a label has been attached, it brings to mind all the characteristics associated with that label, and thus a chance encounter with the word can suddenly summon up a full background of texts and treatises, books and lectures, all of which may or may not be relevant, depending upon how accurate was the labelling in the first place and the extent to which the general characteristics of the label apply in each particular case.

We find that people are labelled as extrovert or introvert; nations as rich or poor; races as black or white. Of course, reality does not divide itself thus neatly into two extremes, but presents us with a whole spectrum of intermediate cases stretching from one extreme to the other. It is the newspapers, the politicians and the advertisers who talk in terms of such extremes, giving us these labels to titillate our senses, to encourage us to vote for this party or buy that product. And we accept them gratefully; we even lap them up. No longer do we need to think; instead we can give full reign to all our preconceptions; we can merely apply the convenient label and then pretend to ourselves that we understand the subject.

This book is concerned with two such labels; Data Base System and Management Information System. Reliance on labelling is often taken to such an extreme that actual words become unnecessary. New, easier words are formed, as in the case of MIS—one word to replace three. But which three? Management Information System? Marketing Information System? System or Services? We now doubly confuse ourselves in thought and conversation, not only with the preconceptions inherent in the full label, but also with the preconceptions of the acronym.

Four themes are recurrent throughout this book. Firstly, there is the theory, which must allow the relevance of individual experience to become apparent to others. The aim, however, is not to present 'ivory tower' theory but to derive theory out of practice.

The second is concerned with practical problems. Theory has a tendency to ignore the irritations of practical problems; if the theory fits most of the time, why bother about the exceptional five per cent? This book is particularly concerned with the practical problems associated with processing data, large volumes of data, since the difficulties of obtaining this data and controlling it and getting it right are often greatly underestimated.

The third subject relates to the manager doing his job, and the information he can use to help him—not the information the theorist thinks he should have, but information he understands and which can help him do the job better.

Finally there is the overriding necessity for the managers, the users, the outside world to take the initiative and use the computer to serve them, to exploit its immense power without being dominated by it.

Technology and its environment

Because of their enormous power we tend to regard computers as something special, and to think of the relationship between computers and the organization as a unique relationship. This is not so, and we can readily trace how the development of computers and their use follows a general pattern of technological progress.

Any new technology brings some change to its environment, and the reactions that follow are the reactions of man towards change. The stages of progress that lead from the development of one new technology to the development of the next follow a trend.

Firstly, a new technology encounters resistance and disbelief. For example, when Alexander Graham Bell met difficulty in raising capital to finance his 'telephone', a leader-writer in a New York paper commented on this with satisfaction, as he felt it indicated the good sense of the people in realizing the impossibility of the human voice being transmitted through a thin copper wire. This is too well known a reaction to need further comment.

In the second stage the technology is used to replace what came before it, in a bigger and better but basically similar way. A good example is found with the early development of the motor car when it was conceived of as a 'horseless carriage'. In the same way computers, when first introduced into the business environment, were used to copy

I Presenting information in graphical form on a standard character set of visual display unit has its limitations, as this photograph of an IBM 2265 Display Station illustrates.

II An ICL 7181 Visual Display Unit.

III An aspect of design work, generating costing information using a lightpen.

the existing punched-card applications; so the idea that you start off by computerizing the payroll is now beginning to raise the same sort of smile that hindsight gives us at the 'horseless carriage'.

The third stage of progress is much more serious. This is where a new language is written and a new discipline created. This is the stage of the enthusiast where the existence of a specialist language accentuates the gulf between the technician and the layman. The following quotation provides an interesting example of such technical language, which can only bewilder the uninitiated.

'For like cause we look to reflexology and its brother feed-back, christened Multiple Closed Loop Servo Theory, for mechanical explanation of Entelechy in Homeostasis and in appetition. This is that governance, whether in living creatures and their societies or in our lively artifacts, that is now called Cybernetics.'

This language problem leads to two abuses: one is talk without understanding, the other is keeping the outsider outside. A real danger is that it becomes very difficult for the outsider to distinguish between the true expert and the charlatan who has the facility to use the language with no real understanding of the subject.

The fourth stage brings understanding. It is at this stage that a new group of people become involved; they come from the outside and take the technology away from the technicians to use it in a practical world. They rely on the technicians for technical advice but they make the technology subservient to the environment and not vice-versa.

The cycle is completed by the fifth stage: a technology has become fully developed, the discipline and language are understood and accepted. After this its use becomes a routine, the rules become a limitation, the innovator becomes frustrated by the restrictions. The change has been accepted so that it is no longer a change but the standard against which any further innovation will be judged. Out of the frustration of the intellectually adventurous comes a new change which starts up the whole cycle again, beginning with 'non-acceptance of the unfamiliar'.

Computers are following this progress: in many organizations they are still somewhere between the second and third stages. This book concerns the fourth stage, the involvement of the outside world, with the users using computers in a new way to do things which could not be done without computers, but at the same time ensuring that their immense potential is kept subservient to the needs of the environment.

17

The language barrier

The ability to communicate through words, to transmit concepts and ideas as well as crude emotions, is a characteristic unique to mankind, and is therefore to be valued. But words can debase as well as ennoble, and if this book is to be properly understood then both author and reader must appreciate the dangers as well as the strength of communication with words, particularly as they are dealing with theories and labels. This section is therefore devoted to the problem of communicating with words. The main purpose in writing this book is to clothe concepts with reality, to bridge the gulf between theory and practice, and this gulf exists partly because of the problems of language. The scientist finds it difficult to communicate with the outside world, and the outside world finds it difficult to differentiate between the scientist and the charlatan.

Three aspects of word usage will be covered here, although, of course, a whole spectrum of such usage exists.

The first aspect is the use of words by experts: technical language used by technical people obsessed with the technology. With grateful acknowledgements to Flanders and Swann, the following extract from *Drop of a Hat* (Parlophone PMCO 1033) illustrates my point exactly:

> You've got your negative feedback
> Coupled in with your push-pull input-output
> Take that across through your red-head pick-up
> To your tweeter. If you're modding more than
> eight, you're going to get wow on your top.
> You try to bring that down through your rumble
> filter to your woofer—what do you get?
> Flutter on your bottom!

To move from the world of entertainment to the world of business, here is an extract from the *Investors' Chronicle and Stock Exchange Gazette* for 24 April 1970:

Digital Gobbledygook
'The Ferranti equipment which is powering the London Stock Exchange's new market price display service is mighty impressive—so impressive in fact, that I didn't understand a word of its technology. The key piece of equipment, which enables subscribers, from their own offices, to get an instant picture of the price movements of the most active stocks, is known as DIGI-TV. It is the vital link between the

feed-in of information to a Ferranti Argus 400 computer and its display on a multi-channel, closed circuit television distribution system.

'A G.P.O. common coaxial land line connects the Stock Exchange to each of the television receivers in the subscribers' offices. This much I can grasp, but I confess to being rapidly out of my depth when I learn that DIGI-TV "time-shares the character generator and control logic among all displays and as a result uses a drum mass data store as a video refresh store". This apparently "relieves the display generator and control logic from work in each display refresh cycle so that they can be time-shared among genuine display data changes to the video refresh store". I could use a refresher course myself.'

Every subject breeds its own enthusiasts, its own experts who rapidly lose sight of the real purpose of the technology or the need to communicate with the outside world. However, these enthusiasts are genuine; they may be removed from reality but at least they know what they are talking about, even if no one else does!

Not so the second aspect of word use, that concerning the charlatan. The charlatan is someone who has a facility to use the words, but with no depth of understanding of the subject involved. The jargon generators of the computer industry have provided fertile ground for the charlatan or the verbal gymnast able to string together buzz words[1] into a meaningless flow of convincing-sounding expertise. 'A pox on the English language' as Clive Jenkins described it.

Of course, this verbal charlatanry is not unique to modern science. All superstitions tend to base their strength on the hocus-pocus of a secret language. Most professions have little need for a trades union, since they have the barrier of their own language which successfully protects them from intrusion and ensures their continued scarcity value. Simple economic concepts can be made confusing by labels such as amortization, D.C.F., liquidity, and wip. Similarly concepts are hidden by lawyers with their long, precise archaic words, and the use of Latin!

The third aspect of word use concerns the non-technical real world, the world experienced in dealing with real events and objects, happenings and people. This real world knows how to cope with situations but not with science, nor with the pseudo science of the charlatan; its reaction resembles that of a research guinea pig towards a frustrated conditioned reflex. This reaction takes one of three forms. When meeting

---

[1] 'Buzz words' is a name given by the jargon generators to jargon. There now appears to be a buzz word for buzz words, 'bunkrupt', coined, I believe, by Paul Jennings.

19

such frustrations the animal either lies down pretending not to notice and goes to sleep; or it rejects the situation, turns its back and walks away; or it battles and tries to master and overcome the cause of its frustration. In our reactions most of us fall into the first two categories. We grow elderly, complacent and lazy and will do our utmost to avoid problems that are difficult to comprehend. Being mental rather than physical, this type of laziness may conceal itself behind a front of activity; doing is so much easier than thinking. It is so much easier to be constantly overworked than to get down to sorting out why, and deciding what needs to be done to avoid the overwork. It is so much more satisfying to be everlastingly busy, to be the king-pin around which everything revolves, than to stop and think. It is so much easier to be everlastingly active, though mentally lazy, than it is to tackle a formless, incomprehensible problem. As a result, the scientists are left alone to develop their own technologies, create their own power and take their own decisions! But do not blame the scientists for Hiroshima, for nerve gases, for irresponsible computer-based credit ratings. Instead blame the mentally lazy, the doers who should be responsible, but prefer a façade of activity to the necessity of thinking.

There are the few who think, who plan, who battle the technology, who come to grips with it, remove its cuckoo-spit of jargon to reveal the heart of it. It is these few imbued with true spirit of the real, sub-jective, emotional world who make a technology effective, who exploit its power in real situations, and until a technology has been accepted by such people it is at best impotent and at worst disastrous.

Language, although, of course, necessary, can also serve as a hind-rance to understanding: one must recognize that the attachment of a label or coining a buzz word usually represents mental laziness, a reluc-tance to think through the subject. The real world can, and must, control the situation, and this control can be achieved with the help of sound common sense and basic English!

It should be possible to analyse the application of computers in the involved subject of management information with similar common sense and freedom from jargon. It is the purpose of this book to show that computer-based management information systems need a foundation of common sense, not technical ideas, and that this is best achieved by peeling away as much jargon as possible from any discussion of the subject.

Chapter 2

The Data Base

Bricks and mortar

This book is concerned with building something that works, and no architect would consider designing a building without full knowledge of the materials available for the task.

Discussions, seminars, lectures, articles and books on management information systems generally tend to ignore the bricks and mortar; they often make the comfortable assumption that a data base exists, is reliable, is readily accessible to the information system, and contains all the data required. This easy let-out is of little value to a man with a job to do; no one up to now has successfully developed anything like the ideal data base with these characteristics, and it is wrong to presume its existence when writing a book on management information systems if this book is to be of any practical value. The concept of the Data Base is expanded later in this book; it is sufficient at this stage to regard it as representing a controlled approach to recording and storing the facts and figures of interest to the organization. The task of creating a Data Base represents a hard, unglamorous slog; the excitement comes later when valid data is readily available and can be freely manipulated, but the following chapters will deal with this hard slog.

Fig. 2.1 presents an analysis undertaken of three returns submitted to the board of directors of a company, and concerned with the value of orders taken by that company in the preceeding twelve months.

The moral is quite clear: here was a board of directors with the responsibility of establishing the future policy of the company, frustrated right at the start by the fact that they did not even know the answer to such a simple question as 'How many orders did we take last year?'. This does not represent a failure in the information system,

ORDERS TAKEN we will define as Customer Orders taken on Permanent Sales Terms to be met by our own manufacturing resources.

At the Managing Director's Committee that met to discuss the year-end returns you had available to you three returns which would appear to answer this question — until one compares the answers.

THE COMPARISON

SUMMARY OF ORDERS RECEIVED AND CANCELLATIONS During twelve months ended 30 September 1971 (excluding miscellaneous items)				
Sales return 7	At sale price £'000 SUMMARY OF ORDERS RECEIVED AND CANCELLED Amount and Programme for year to date ex order form	Total orders taken	Outstanding orders cancelled	NET ORDERS TAKEN
		29,338	4,678	24,660

ANALYSIS OF PERMANENT ORDERS RECEIVED During twelve months ended 30 September 1971. Based on order forms, values in terms of £'000s of standard works costs.		
Sales return 12		TOTAL SALE AND OWN USE
N.B. Local manufacturing included under appropriate sales terms.	GRAND TOTAL	13,827

SUMMARY OF DEMAND AND SUPPLY ON PERMANENT SALES TERMS (Excluding local sources) up to the end of September 1971 (in £'000s of works costs).		
Manufacturing return 3c		ORDERS ACCEPTED
	Total	12,960
	Deliveries for own use	73
	Sales to the trade	1,502
	TOTAL	14,535

We have gone through a complicated process of deduction and algebraic substitution and have come to the following conclusion:

THE VALUE OF PERMANENT CUSTOMER ORDERS TAKEN (OTHER THAN THOSE TO BE MET BY LOCAL MANUFACTURING) DURING YEAR ENDED 30 SEPTEMBER 1971 AT STANDARD WORKS COSTS

£13,205,000 ± £70,000

But if the truth were known —   NOBODY KNOWS!

Fig. 2.1

however, but a failure in the bricks and mortar. This example is not unique to that particular company. There must be many boards who find their meetings devoted to wrangling over conflicting figures rather than discussing matters of policy. Such situations, which one can highlight, as I have done, at board level, extend all the way through an organization, and it is this symptom of conflicting returns which demonstrates the disease of uncontrolled data. The cure is a ready access to controlled, reliable data; the provision of such data is the subject of the next few chapters.

There are those who argue that it is necessary to conceive of and design the management information system before one starts establishing the data base. One should, they say, conduct an exhaustive survey of a company and its managers to find out what information they use now and what information they think they need to have in order to do their job properly. Having done this, one should then set about establishing the data base to serve these identified information needs. I do not share this view!

Whilst clearly a limited amount of preliminary work is necessary, to believe that one can anticipate *now* what the information needs will be in three to four years' time, when the data base has been established, is to close one's eyes to the essential dynamics of the situation—the dynamics brought about by the ever-changing environment and those brought about by the developing experience of the managers themselves. Part of the bricks and mortar therefore is the need for a foundation that can be used to meet an ever-changing situation.

The man who was ideally suited to stone-age living would be very ill-equipped to cope with the present times. The evolutionary process is a dual affair: man changes his environment, and the environment changes man. Management activity is similarly evolving, and recognition of this evolutionary process is the first hurdle to be overcome by those engaged in developing management and information systems. Certain physical characteristics of man have not changed, although they may have adapted themselves—arms and legs, alimentary canal, and so forth. There are certain patterns of mental activity that have not changed: man's ability to develop conditioned reflexes; to learn by experience, both consciously and unconsciously; to develop technologies; and to react emotionally. All these are therefore facets of the developing situation within which a management information system needs to operate.

Three 'bricks and mortar' subjects need to be discussed. The first is Data, the second is codes, and the third is Processing.

Categories of data

Data is a fancy name for facts and figures; it represents the raw material which is processed to produce an output: invoices, bills of lading, rating demands, reports and management information in general. One can divide the data required for a management information system into two major groups. First there is data concerned with day-to-day operations: internal data arising out of the normal operational activities. Secondly there is external data relating to the environment in which the organization is operating: economic trends, market patterns, competitive activity, and so forth.

This book is primarily concerned with the former group, although reference is made to the latter where appropriate. This is because an organization needs above all to have details of what is going on inside it. Control of normal day-to-day operational data is a big step forward for most organizations and its ready availability will satisfy the bulk of information requirements; although in certain areas of activity, notably market and corporate planning, external data also plays an important part.

Data can be divided quite readily into three categories, and it is necessary to establish disciplined demarcations between these three for their successful control. First there is the quantifiable operational data that arises out of those of the organization's activities which are normally subjected to precise accounting-type disciplines—the data associated with pay and invoicing or stock control for example. In order to fulfil their functions adequately, the managers concerned have a responsibility and a vested interest in ensuring that the data is absolutely correct; routines for balancing are well established, check totals exist at every stage, and in general the tools for controlling the data are in common usage.

The second category of data has the precise, numeric characteristic associated with the first, but it has not traditionally been subjected to the same disciplines. This is particularly the case with certain types of external data whose application is purely for information, having no direct involvement in a line operation. There is a great danger in attempting to subject this sort of data to the same rigorous control as operational data, but, on the other hand, the information system needs to know very clearly the degree of reliance it can place upon it. One can very easily fall into the trap of deciding to establish a data control function for this sort of data, and man it with staff having an accounting background. They will instinctively attempt to control all quantifiable

PROBLEM: Prepare a revenue forcast for the next twelve months

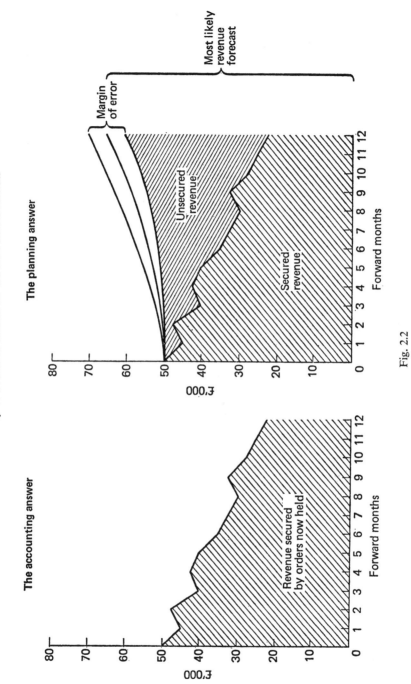

Fig. 2.2

25

data with accounting disciplines and can rapidly evolve a mammoth and frustrating operation intent on trying to control the uncontrollable. Far better to identify the extent to which control can be exercised, ensuring that where necessary it really is one hundred per cent correct, rather than dissipate effort where it is not needed. The difficulty is that an accountant is not trained to discriminate in this way; if faced with a set of figures his reaction is to check and double check, balance and cross balance. The discretion needs to be exercised by the prime user of the data: only he is aware of the value to him of its accuracy. This situation is very often illustrated by the presentation of forecast information. Fig. 2.2 shows two forecasts, the first based on known, factual, correct, accounting information, whilst the second is prepared by a prime user using his discretion.

The third category of data is descriptive or non-quantifiable. Whilst it needs to be available it cannot be controlled by normal numeric disciplines: for example, name and address, product specification, and so forth. This is in many ways the most difficult category of data, as it is often essential for it to be correct, but it is very difficult to establish reliable updating routines.

There is another characteristic which separates each of these three categories of data into two sub-groupings, and that is the extent to which there is a line executive with an active vested interest in the accuracy of the data. For example, market researchers might well want information on all customer names and addresses. If the name and address provided is the one used by the accountants for invoicing, then they can have considerable confidence in its accuracy. If, however, it is the name and address used for distributing promotional material, then there is much less room for confidence.

Three levels of data need to be considered. The first can be called 'current status'. This represents the most up-to-date statement of the state of that particular aspect of data. The second level can be called the 'historical trail': this is the record of all the events that have led up to the 'current status'. The third level represents indexing data, that is data which is common to more than one statement. For example, each order for product A will have its own records on the file showing the current status (and if appropriate its historical trail), but all the records concerned with product A require certain standard or indexing data: price, product description, and so forth. It is clearly more effective to control this index data by its appearance once only on an index than by accessing every record in which product A appears. Indexing data will of course often have current status and historical trail levels (current price and previous price for example), and one of the problems associ-ated with the use of index files is to ensure compatibility in time scale between an entry on the historical trail of the index and an entry on the historical trail of the main file.

It may be helpful to summarize these various subdivisions of data.

(a) Two major groupings of data required by an organization:
1. Internal.
2. External.

(b) Three categories of data exist within each group:
1. Quantifiable operational data subject to precise disciplines in normal operations.
2. Quantifiable data not normally subjected to precise disciplines.
3. Non-quantifiable data.

(c) Two characteristics:
1. A line executive exists whose operation absolutely depends upon the accuracy of the data.
2. Such an executive does not exist.

(d) Three levels of data:
1. Current status.
2. Historical trail.
3. Indexing.

Any data situation contains a mixture of the items listed above which represent the various aspects of data needing to be examined.

The reality of data

Merleau-Ponty in his *The Phenomenology of Percephim* (translated by Jonathan Benthall) wrote:

'The unrolling of sensible data before our eyes or our hands is like a language that teaches itself, whose significance is secreted by the very structure of the signs, and that is why one can say literally that our senses interrogate things and things reply to our senses. . . .'

The reality of data is well illustrated by the following case history. At the normal monthly Board Meeting of XYZ Ltd, discussion centred around the apparent failure of the Production Director to meet his output target. The figures presented by the Director of Finance showed quite clearly that the value of output in the past quarter was ten per cent below target. As the order situation was very healthy, this was causing the Managing Director grave concern and he castigated the Production Director accordingly. The Production Director was furious;

27

using good engineering language he commented that one never could trust these accountants' figures, that he had achieved his output targets and that the Director of Finance (was an ignorant b.....d and) did not know what he was talking about. The Board Meeting then rapidly degenerated into a wrangle over the figures and the Managing Director was hard pressed to restore order and proceed into calmer waters.

The irony of this situation was that it was the Production Director who was right and the problem was one of understanding the reality of data. The situation in the works which gave rise to this conflict was as follows.

When the Works Manager completed an item in his output programme, he passed it to the warehouse where it was held pending receipt of an order with packaging and despatch information. As far as he was concerned it was made and was in stock. The warehouse manager shared this view, which was anyway patently true because you could go and touch it, count it, kick it! It was there. It was real. According to established routines, the works manager compiled his monthly reports of how many items he had manufactured and passed these to the Production Director.

The Cost Accountant in the same factory received dockets concerning the man-hours spent and the materials used in manufacturing this product. He calculated the direct costs attributable to it, loaded it with appropriate overheads and indirect costs, and compiled the accounts for the factory, showing the value of output, stocks and so forth. According to established routines, the Cost Accountant compiled his monthly reports and passed these to the Finance Director.

The day of the board meeting arrives and the two directors meet with the disastrous consequences detailed earlier. The output programme had been achieved all right, but there was a time-lag in compiling the accounts, so final cost figures were not yet available to the Cost Accountant for some of the items in stock. His routines would not permit him to show the item if he could not show the cost; the reality of the existence of the product in stock was obscured by the paper-work processes which only identified 'realities' if preceded by a £ sign.

The true reality was that the items were completed and were in stock, and it is essential when considering data to identify such realities. The data realities of the cost accounting information are the details of the man-hours spent and materials used; the accountant then processes this data to produce the information concerning the cost of the product.

28

One can always qualify the recording of the data, the true reality, by saying that the cost accounting information is not yet available for some of the items that are in stock; and routines can be developed to apply notional or average values to them. However, one must never deny the reality of the data.

Data therefore is concerned with real events happening to real things. It is surprising how few real things there are in any organization, and the process of identifying the real events that happen to them is an exercise of common sense.

In order to give substance to another technical term 'Data Base', (which has already been used several times in this book) it is necessary to pause and reflect on the way files of data have developed over the years. Any manager over the years accumulates records which he uses to help him fulfil his responsibilities. The data he collected in these records was rightly aimed specifically at supporting the particular applications for which he was responsible—any other data was rigorously excluded. He developed for himself routines to ensure that the data flowed adequately to update his records, and he conscientiously strove to ensure that the records he used were as accurate as possible. Thus in any organization, as the years go by, numerous data files are assembled by individual managers and used by them to fulfil the applications for which they are responsible. This proliferation of application-oriented data files, however, produced problems whenever it became necessary to relate or compare one function with another. Several files might receive simultaneous notification of a particular event but they might well deal with it differently, for example, by using different definitions to classify the event and different codes in identifying it. An organization might use the notification of the despatch to a customer of the machines it manufactured to trigger off a number of consequential actions. One copy of the despatch notification goes to the accounting people for invoicing purposes, one to the stock controller for inventory purposes, one to the salesman concerned to let him know that his customer should be receiving the product, one to the sales statistics department to inform them that an order has now been satisfied, and finally one to the technical branch who keep records of the whereabouts of all the machines in case of complaint. Each function has a different interest and so concentrates on different aspects of the despatch data. Thus even in this simple case, five data files are being independently updated according to different disciplines. An attempt to compare or reconcile these five different files would be fraught with difficulties and could produce many non-matching records.

29

Complications often arise. For example, the customer might not accept delivery for some reason, or perhaps the salesman, in response to a particularly urgent selling situation, might intercept that despatch and divert it to another customer. Another possibility is that the customer would accept delivery and pay for the machine, but subsequently he might re-sell it to a third party. These types of situation, where dealt with at all, might be handled quite differently according to the efficiency of the data flow and the needs of the data file. It might be essential for the invoicing department to know if a despatch to one customer has been switched to another, but this is of no significance to the stock controller who has recorded it as being despatched to the first customer. The technical branch might strive to keep track of each item and seek information if one customer resold it to another, but the invoicing department would have no interest in this.

The maze set out above is still basically quite a simple one; far more complex situations exist in most organizations, and yet even this simple one creates havoc for any attempt to provide a full picture of what has happened to each item despatched, or any total statement of 'how many'.

It is into this complexity that one is able to introduce the simple concept of a real event happening to a real thing. Accepting this concept, one can readily trace a sequence of real events that happen to these real machines, and it becomes axiomatic that tremendous benefits would ensue from having only one source of information about these events which would provide for each application area the elements of data they required. In the example given, the despatch notification would go to this source as would the notification of all the other events. The file held there would be updated and would feed to each application the elements of data needed for that application.

In the last few pages historically-developed application-oriented data files have been contrasted with the concept of providing a master updating location for each element of data in a data base, and using this data base for all the applications.

A further case history adds a touch of realism which illustrates admirably the contrast between the tidy concept of 'a real event happening to a real thing' and the normal confusions of the world. A non-executive director of XYZ Ltd, who was also the Managing Director of another company with whom they did a lot of business, asked to be told about the XYZ Ltd 'information system'. Proudly this was displayed. It included a computer-produced 'Trading Directory' listing all the organizations with whom XYZ Ltd had a trading interest, and also specific locations in those organizations—it might be the location where equipment was installed, or where the accounts should be sent, or the head office, and so forth. The firm of which he was Managing Director was represented by about twenty entries, as it had a number of factories where XYZ products were used. He examined the list with great interest and, with the malicious joy of mankind in the misfortunes of others, he pointed to one of the entries and said, 'We closed that factory eighteen months ago.' Embarrassed silence ensued; some sort of feeble excuse was offered and a new topic of conversation was frantically sought!

However, on further investigation, it was discovered that not only was that location recorded as one in which XYZ Ltd *currently* had a trading interest, but three months previously they had sent his firm an invoice for maintenance work undertaken there ... and one month previously his firm had paid it!

Subsequent study established that honours were even and that there was a logical explanation for this mix up. It was true that the firm had closed that factory; they had moved the smaller items of equipment themselves but had asked XYZ engineers to move the larger items. The records held by XYZ Ltd therefore showed that the larger items were now in a new location, but they made no reference to a change in location for the smaller ones. As far as this director's accounts were concerned, he still owned all the equipment, so its location was immaterial to paying the invoice.

This, then illustrates some of the 'bricks and mortar' data problems— or the importance of a proper understanding and control over the data to be used in an information system.

Although such terms as 'elements of data' and 'data base' have been used, the word 'computer' has not yet appeared in this section. This was quite deliberate, because this chapter is not about computers, but about data. The logic of data and of data control is self-supporting and does not need talk of computers to support it. What is so magic about computers anyway? Real events happen to real things, and it is quite possible to have a master updating location for recording these without using a computer. What mysterious powers does the computer have that invalidates any master updating locations not held on a computer?

The problem to be considered relates to the data of an organization, *all* the relevant data regardless of the means by which it is stored. Obviously, computers provide a very useful tool for storing, retrieving and processing this data, but an obsession with the technology of this tool rapidly clouds the simplicity of the concept.

So far this chapter has demonstrated the reality of data; it has defined elements of data as records of a real event happening to a real thing, and a data base as providing a master updating location for each element. It is now intended to explore in more depth the problem of ensuring the validity of this data, before (in the next section) describing in some detail the operation of a particular data base.

It is clearly essential, if one is to construct a data base, that great care has to be exercised in ensuring the validity of the data. If there is going to be only one source for this data one loses the means of testing its validity against other data files. With a data base, if the data is wrong, then every application using that data will be wrong.

Although this problem is increasingly recognized, controlled solutions are rarely found. In business activities an error in a data base may result in wrong invoices, accounts, stock records and such like; but where the data base is concerned with records about people an error in the data base can result in human tragedy. Most of us are reluctant to admit that we are already active partners in a society that lives on credit. A central data base providing traders with information on our credit rating could do us great harm if, perhaps through some punching error, our record showed us to be not credit-worthy. Nobody, from building societies to banks, would be prepared to lend us anything. Similar problems arise when an organization maintains comprehensive personnel records on a data base and uses that data base to select suitable candidates as vacancies arise. The errors that can occur result not only from straightforward operational mistakes—coding or punching errors, transcribing errors, checking errors—but also, where input data originates in a large number of different locations, they can result from different interpretations of the input disciplines. The following is an example of this. An H.Q. personnel unit was using details of employee qualifications to select candidates for vacancies, quite unaware that individual personnel officers around the organization were using quite different disciplines to control the input of qualification information; some even were not including it at all, or only in a very haphazard way.

It is necessary to trap data elements at the time the events happen and to receive them from the people causing them to happen. Further, the process of trapping this data should not impose on these people a burden in which they have no vested interest. A data base is not something that can be superimposed upon an operation: it must become an integral part of that operation. Nothing brings failure more quickly to a potential data base than a situation where the people causing these

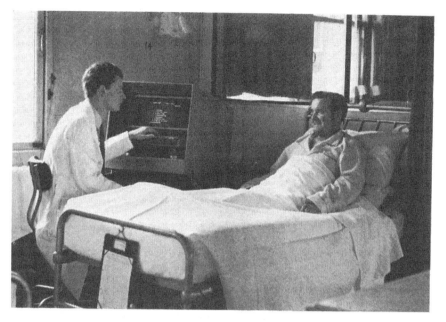

IV A doctor using a V.D.U. to access a patient's medical record.

V An interactive display unit being used in design work.

VI   An IBM 3277 Model 2 Visual Display station typically used as an inquiry station in a management information system.

innumerable small events to happen have to say to themselves, 'Oh, yes, I must remember to tell the data base I have done so-and-so.' Sometimes they will not remember! And anyway, if they do remember, they have no vested interest in ensuring that the data they provide is correct.

There are many methods of ensuring the validity of the data; two of them will be described here but they should not be regarded as the only ones.

First of all it is valuable to exploit a person's self-interest. A salesman needs to record the fact that he has taken an order to ensure that goods will be delivered to his customer, and also to ensure that he will receive the credit or commission due to him. The salesman is not interested, however, in recording the details of the orders he has taken merely in order to update the data base. One must design the reporting procedures the salesman has to adopt in order to ensure delivery and commission so that they also supply the data required by the data base; and the data-base routines must be designed to accept inputs that are not designed specifically for data-updating purposes, but for the operational requirements of the individuals originating them. It is much easier to impose a self-discipline on how one interprets and processes the input, than to ensure that many individuals will supply data in a special content and format which is of no value to them for their immediate purpose.

The second approach is so to design the system that it cannot operate without the data base being updated; the process of updating the data base then becomes an essential part of the overall operation for which a person is responsible. If the data base is not updated with the data for which he is responsible, then he cannot do his job. This approach is illustrated in the next section.

Case study: a data base on personnel

This particular case study is presented here because it embraces many principles of data-base management and operations. Where not dealt with earlier, these principles will be explored in the context of this specific example.

A fundamental misconception about a data base is that it is a vast random-access computer file in the centre of a company, containing all —whatever 'all' is—the data of the company, and into which anyone can dip at will in order to obtain some information required. And so this data base should contain the one and only statement for each element of data, which need not, and indeed must not, be repeated elsewhere.

33

The fallacy in this concept has already been emphasized by demonstrating that a data base is concerned with the data of a company rather than with data on a computer. It has also been suggested that an essential ingredient in ensuring the validity of the data is the involvement of the data base in the day-to-day operations of the company. IIC Ltd, whose personnel data base will be described, is geographically widely spread, not just in one country, but throughout the world.

Technically, of course, it would be feasible to link all locations with wide-band data-transmission highways, and satellite transmission, thereby making possible the concept of a central file involved in the day-to-day operations in each location, but the costs of such links would throw into question the whole economic viability of such an operation.

A further general point to consider is the way a data base provides data for a whole range of applications. No longer can one view each individual item of data as related to only one application: it may well be used in a large number of applications. The information that appears in a personnel data base about an employee's salary is certainly used for the payroll routine, and payroll is an important application of a personnel data base; but the same information would also be used in costing and budgeting, activity reporting, manpower planning, wage negotiations, statistical analysis, and any other application at either the operational level or the summary level where information on salaries may be required.

Having isolated two of the fundamental problems to be overcome, the geographic problem and the multitudinous uses of a data base, the case study is now presented so as to illustrate how these particular problems were overcome.

In order to construct a data base that overcomes the geographic problem, and allows for regional variations but at the same time provides the means for corporate interrogation and manipulation, the basic record for each employee on the computer may be considered as being divided into three parts. The first part identifies the employee by his personnel number. The second part contains data using a common format and common coding throughout IIC Ltd: name, address, location, annual salary, job classification, qualifications, and so forth. The third part contains data that is unique to the operational requirements of each location. This is illustrated in Fig. 2.3.

As far as each location is concerned, the whole file acts as its source of data for the various personnel administration and payroll applications requiring it; thus each location has its own data base on personnel. At

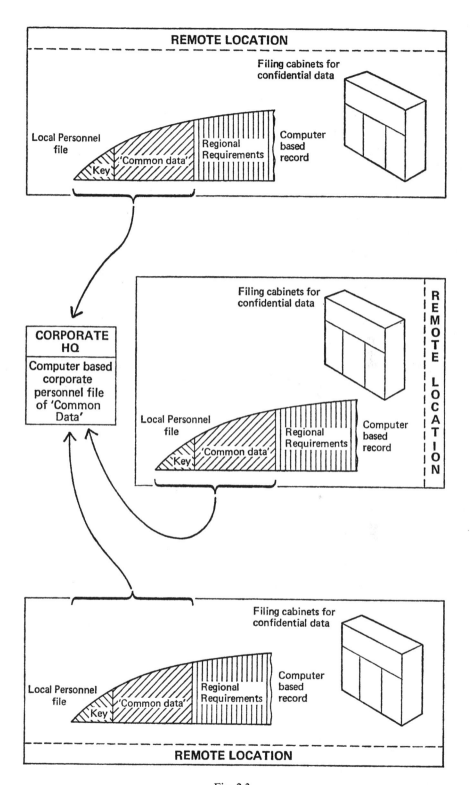

Fig. 2.3

the same time, the facility exists for taking the first two parts of the record from each location and updating a central corporate data base.

This corporate file can be used for corporate personnel functions: manpower planning and development, corporate statistics, statutory returns and individual employee searches. These corporate functions do not require day-by-day updating, and it is quite adequate to update the corporate file on a monthly basis. The essential discipline, however, is that elements of data cannot be introduced or changed at the corporate level: the remote operational file provides their master updating location.

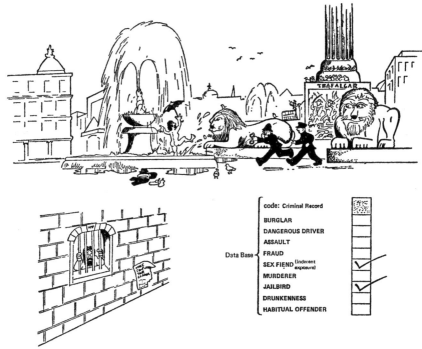

Fig. 2.4

The problem of recording and codifying confidential personnel information is one causing grave concern to many people at the moment. The strip cartoon (Fig. 2.4) illustrates the fanciful but not unrealistic problem of how to record the fact that, as an irresponsible undergraduate in his youth, a company employee spent one night in jail for bathing naked in a fountain in Trafalgar Square. The final picture presents the quandary of the coding clerk, who has to decide, from the limited choice in the code book, how to cope with this situation.

Although jail for one night as a result of a youthful escapade is not very serious, and is unlikely to be a relevant consideration when deciding how to employ someone, jail for three years as a result of fraud is quite a different matter.

The range of potential data elements concerned with confidential individual personnel information is vast: peculiar marital status (three current wives and five little children), has written a best-selling novel, and so on. It is clearly necessary that this sort of information should be available but it can be argued that it should not be codified and recorded on a computer file. The personnel data base described copes with this situation by recording this type of information in an ordinary file in an ordinary filing cabinet and identifying the location of this file by a code on the computer record. Thus this filing cabinet is absolutely part of the data base, providing the master updating location for this category of data.

It can be seen from what has been described so far that this personnel data base is truly concerned with all the data on an employee, rather than just computer data, and that it is made up of filing cabinets, operational files in various locations, and a corporate file held centrally. This demonstrates clearly the logical organization of data required for a data base, with a master updating location for each data element.

Earlier reference was made to the necessity of involving the data base in the day-to-day activities of the organization in order to ensure the validity of the data; and it was stated that one approach to this was to design the system in such a way that it would not operate without constant updating of the data base. The system used as the basis for this case study is very flexible; it allows for regional variations and it illustrates this close involvement very well. The detailed operation of this aspect of the system is described below.

When designing the system the corporate personnel authorities felt that the changes requiring data to be updated were most likely to be generated by three groups of people: the employee himself, his manager, and his personnel officer. The system has been designed around these three people and in each case an essential ingredient to the system is a turn-round document, generated by the computer, which is used to notify any change. It is called the Personnel Record and Advice Form (PRAF) (Fig. 2.5), and is the one used by the employee's manager. As he is the person most likely to originate a change in the data, the routine he follows will be described in detail.

The PRAF has been designed to be the basic personnel record held by the manager for all the employees who report to him. In most cases

37

IIC PERSONNEL RECORD AND ADVICE FORM

	I.P.P. centre	Date of run
	1A1	11/01/71

MR. M.J. FLOWERS
100001

	Job titles	Dates	Grades	Dates				P/W paid	Annual salary
PERS OFFICER(SYSTEMS)	23 07 69	1P05	23 07 69				P	1768 0
PERSONNEL OFFICER	13 04 67	1P04	13 04 67			Notice 04	All'ce code	Allowances 91 0

Reason 3 2						E.I.T.B. code 5			Leave days 20
Locations 1000143 1000437 1000104					Building LON24		Expense scale C	Leave scale 3
		304	289	327				User code 2	Car allowance

Dates 22 07 69 / 23 07 69 Reason 3 2
Dates 23 07 69 / 13 04 67 Reason 3 2

Date of joining	Calculated date	Date of birth	Date of next review	Review code	Hours			C.S.S.	Date raised	Sick scheme	R.D. code
01 09 58	04 06 54	11 11 11	01 11 70	1	3700		314		12 03 69		W

NIIP PLAN12345 21 015 / 2

Address: 56 CARETON RD TUFFNEL PARK N 12

Category 4 Release code Rx S/M/W. M Foreign languages FRE GER 3

Personal file ref. P Potential 2 D70 C73 Personal ref. 569

Performance XL Test results X073 Dates 14 06 69

Special notes
COMPUTER LIASON IN PERS ADMIN

Training qualifications and experience
SCH CERT (MATRIC) STUDENT MBR IPM, STAFF DUTIES
CRSE 1964. WIDE EXP OF IND RELATIONS, TOOK PART IN
FAWLEY NEGOTIATIONS 1959, BCS PART 1 1969

Changes and recommendations

Manager	Date	Approval	Date	Personnel unit	Date	Personnel unit

Date of run 11/01/71

Name MR M J FLOWERS
Personal No. 100001
Location 1000143
Building LON24

Card type		Amend't type	Personal number	Leavers code	Date of Birth	Amending date		Basic annual salary	Amount	Punch in all cards	Card type	Amend't type	Reason	Perform-ance	Date of review	Review code	C.S.S.	Expense scale	Leave scale	User code	Date rated		Weekly hours	Leave days	Notice period	I.P.P. centre	Location reason	Re-emp. code	Date of location change	Date of leaving	Location		Terminal reason
EC		23	100001	7 8	11 11 11			01768 00	+0156 00	23 10 69	DC	14	XL	01 11 70	569 D70 C73	1	314	C	3	2	12 03 69		3700	20	04	1A1	3		22 10 69		1000143	
FC		23				23 10 69		0091 00	0025 00	M			XL	16 03 69	569	2	314		2													

it is the only record he holds. It is generated when an employee first joins the company and updated versions follow his subsequent career. The task of a manager, when transferring from one responsibility to another, is greatly eased in that he has a readily accessible source of information on all his new staff, presented in a uniform way whatever his job; and equally, when an employee moves from one job to another, his documentation automatically follows him.

The PRAF is divided into three sections, separated by perforations; these sections are comprised of the top (A), middle (B) and lower (C) sections. Section A is a straightforward print-out of relevant fields from the data base; in addition to current status data, historical trail data is shown for such things as job classification, annual salary changes, and so forth. Space is available for up to three historical entries printed out for all the items in the top two complete lines of section A. This top section acts as the personnel record and is the reference document for the manager. Further historical information is, of course, available on request.

Section B is the action section. When the manager wishes to implement some change to the employee's status, award him a salary increase perhaps, or transfer him to another location, he writes down in this centre section what he wants to do. The computer aspects of the system do not constrain him in the way he expresses his intentions, the only constraint being the requirements of the personnel authorities. For example they might well insist that a salary increase of more than, say, £250 needs to be countersigned by a more senior manager. Having written his intention in the centre section, he detaches sections B and C from section A, sends B and C to his personnel control unit, and retains A in his file.

The personnel control unit examines what the manager has written, to ensure that it conforms with company policy; and then they code section C. Coding is made as simple as possible as the computer has already printed out details of the relevant information above a dotted line. The coding function has to enter the details of any new data below any data that is changed. If a figure is not changed no coding action is taken. Sections B and C are then separated; B remains with the personnel unit as their authority for what has been done, and Section C goes for data preparation. Punching simply involves punching the key to identify the employee, and the details of any coded change. Once punched, the cards are fed into the computer; the data base as updated and this updating generates all the consequential actions that follow the change being notified—if the change relates to salary, for example, the payroll routines are initiated. An updated version of the PRAF is produced which goes back to the manager, who files it until the next time he wishes to make a change.

Fig. 2.6 *a*

"For any substantial change an output is produced, containing details of the change, and this goes to the employee himself." Figure 2.6 *a* is an example of this.

For any substantial change an output is produced, containing details of the change, and this goes to the employee himself, who is asked to check it for errors or queries. Even if no change has been notified, each employee is given a statement of the computer record once a year so that he can satisfy himself that no misleading information about him is held on the computer, and also as a reminder to him to notify the company of any changes in his personal circumstances of which they might not otherwise be aware.

Two minor aspects of the system are worthy of comment. The manner in which confidential data is dealt with has been described already: the Personnel File Reference Number appears on Section A and this leads the manager to the source of confidential information about that employee if he wishes to refer to it.

Security is always a problem with a personnel system; one small aspect is illustrated on the PRAF which shows that although the employee's name and number appears on Sections A and B, only the

---

IIC THE INTERNATIONAL
INGESTOR CORPORATION **LTD**

TO: MR. M. J. FLOWERS   DATE: 30/10/71

LON 11   REF. NO. 1A1/472/100001

WE ARE SURE YOU WOULD LIKE TO HAVE A NOTE OF THE MAJOR

DETAILS CONCERNING YOURSELF WHICH ARE HELD ON THE

COMPUTERISED PERSONNEL RECORDS. WE IN TURN WOULD BE

GRATEFUL IF YOU WOULD CHECK THE LIST GIVEN BELOW AND

LET YOUR MANAGER KNOW OF ANY DISCREPANCY.

ADDRESS	21 SOUTH DRIVE, EALING W.5.		
JOB TITLE	PERSONNEL OFFICER		
PERSONAL NO.	100001		
ANNUAL SALARY	£2432.04	ANNUAL ALLOWANCE	£104.00
EXPENSE SCALE	C	NOTICE PERIOD	4 WEEKS
LEAVE SCALE	4	LEAVE DAYS	20
LOCATION CODE	472	WEEKLY HOURS	37.00
STATUS	SINGLE	N.I. NUMBER	TY673216D
DATE OF BIRTH	010101	DATE OF JOINING	25/12/70

Fig. 2.6 b

From time to time, at least once a year, the output illustrated in
2.6 b is produced for each employee detailing the main items on
his personnel record and asking him to check their accuracy.

personnel number appears on Section C, thus as soon as the sections
of the PRAF go beyond the manager or the personnel officer, employees
are identified by number only.

Clearly in any system dealing with a large number of employees,
various sub-routines need to exist to cater for block changes rather than

individual changes; a routine exists for wage awards, for example, and thus there are other ways of updating the data base than by completing a PRAF.

The routine associated with the use of the PRAF has been described so as to demonstrate clearly how the updating of the data base is an absolutely integral part of operating the system.

The data base has been designed for use in the normal day-to-day operations of the organization, and there are a number of people, the manager, the personnel officers and the employee himself, directly involved in maintaining the accuracy of the data.

Management information in its many forms is absolutely dependent upon a reliable source of data, a data base containing accurate information about the day-to-day operations, and the personnel data base described in the case study provides just that.

Chapter 3

Data Processing

Change

Thus far the nature of data has been described, and also the principles of marshalling data into a data base. The fundamental nature of data—real events happening to real things—is valid for most situations, regardless of context. In local government one is dealing with 'plots of land', ratepayers, corporation vehicles, employees. In the armed services one is dealing with men, with fighting units, with basic items of ordnance and supplies, with locations or establishments, with vehicles, staff, and so forth. In commerce there are products, customers and suppliers, employees, materials. In transportation there are seats, vehicles or aircraft, points of call, harbours, airports, bus stops, employees. The list is endless, but in each set of circumstances it is possible to isolate the important 'real things' which are significant to that particular organization.

The intention, however, is to present a concept of a data base that can become a reality, not just another statement of arid theory, and reality presents one dominant constraint which cannot be ignored: and this is change—change of circumstances, the environment, level of understanding, people. In real life all these are constantly changing, so acceptance of perpetual change is an essential ingredient for any data-base system. The system must be designed to expect change, to accept change as part of the system, not as something the system rejects.

This problem of accepting change becomes even more acute with an operation which is geared to use a data base. What happens if the data base is wrongly organized and cannot be adapted to meet new situations? All the systems using that data then become affected.

The next sections deal with three aspects of planning for change. One case only deals specifically with computer techniques; the other two are of more general concern.

43

The history and language of processing

This book has earlier touched on the historical progress in computing. A common thread present in all aspects of computing, to a greater or lesser extent, is the processing of data, but of course the problems of data processing are not new. As long as there has been data, it has needed processing, and there has been data ever since man entered into community activity.

There are two facets to data processing. There are the problems associated with moving data about, managing the data but not affecting the basic nature of each element of data; and there is the doing of things to that data, things which directly affect its value or identity.

The problems associated with processing data are not new; the languages and symbols may change, new and powerful devices may become available, but they all have to deal with fundamentally similar problems. To illustrate this point, here is a list of some basic data-processing activities:

Accepting data and checking that it is right.
Sorting it into sequence.
Comparing one piece of data with another.
Selecting particular bits of data from a mass.
Collating two sets of data.
Copying data.
Combining two data records with common identifiers.
Performing mathematical functions on a selection of data.
Presenting the data in a form that can be read and used.

To some measure the punched-card machines, now so much looked down upon, recognized these functions and developed special machines to reflect them:

Sorters to sort data.
Collators to collate data.
Reproducers to copy or combine data.
Calculators to perform mathematical functions.
Tabulators to present readable and usable results.

A manager dealing with a body of data would develop a punch-card file to contain the data he required, and would use this to help him fulfil the application for which he was responsible. He would have available clearly established data-processing techniques, as identified by the machines in his machine room, and so his thinking on data-processing problems could readily encompass the basic techniques. As companies grew, so punch-card rooms proliferated, and within each machine room there would be a number of application-oriented data files.

The advent of the computer in this situation was not altogether happy. We have already seen how a new technology becomes perverted to conform to previously understood disciplines, and the early task given to computers was to computerize the previous punch-card application.

A new breed of specialist employee emerged: the programmer. He knew a lot about the computer and the language by which one could communicate with the computer, but very little about the fundamentals of processing data. The result was that individual programs were written for each of the previous punch-card applications, fulfilling the applications as they had been previously fulfilled, but not recognizing the basic similarities between the processing undertaken for each individual application. Certain basic functions were identified: initially, sorting and, subsequently, simple selection and report generation, but apart from these the developments in computerization followed the application rather than the processing. Even today the most readily accepted aspects concern application: software houses and manufacturers offer innumerable application packages.

There were some benefits deriving from this early computerization activity: processing was speeded up; clerical effort was saved. However, a price had to be paid, and that was the very considerable investment demanded in programming: whereas a tabulator could be adapted to satisfy a new application or data format merely by replugging, a computer had to be re-programmed, and so its flexibility proved an illusion. A new breed of experts emerged, dedicated to the computer and the task of making the computer work as efficiently as possible—with fantastic speeds, sophisticated calculations. What suffered was the business itself: the tail was wagging the dog. As one executive put it, 'Even to breathe you have to quote a six digit number, and you haven't enough breath left for that . . .'

There followed a period of even greater confusion. The computer men began to realize their failure to serve the business; to redeem the balance, 'integrated systems' became their watch-word. Each individual application was carefully interfaced with the other applications so as to build a delicate card house of precisely linked systems. Such great care was taken to ensure that all appropriate points were linked that any change at any point could well create a mammoth task of reprogramming; the computer staff multiplied, system maintenance became their dominant activity, and their new cry was, 'Don't change the

45

system. Please don't change the system!' Unfortunately, business is not a static institution: to survive it must be dynamic, it must react rapidly to a changing market place; and instead of being its servant, the computer with its language and disciplines became a millstone. Many companies are still in this stage; and as time passes, so increases their investment in a highly involved, frequently patched network of integrated systems, and their dependence on the few computer staff who really know how it works becomes frightening. Documentation lags, disenchantment sets in, the overworked computer staff leave, and the business suddenly finds itself with a crisis—a data crisis.

The lesson to be learnt is that computer activity must be made flexible; it must be made to serve the company. The common denominator is to be found in the fundamentals of processing. It is not just that one payroll is like another payroll, but that the data-processing functions already listed are to be found in various combinations in all systems, be they payroll, inventory management, sales ledger, or any other activity concerned with processing data.

The computer professionals are now becoming increasingly aware of these fundamentals. An application problem need no longer be viewed in isolation as requiring a unique solution. Rather it is considered as a requirement for data and the processing of that data. Software facilities are now becoming available which fulfil the tasks of managing and processing data. Thus the solution for an application can be found by selecting the most appropriate facilities and by describing the data which the application uses. Instead of a highly technical programmer writing a complex application program, an analyst can concentrate upon understanding the business and the problems of the business. With this understanding, and supported by the availability of facilities for managing and processing data, he can prepare a solution by exploiting the computer, without the intervention of any application programs.

It follows that new problems, or changes to existing problems, can be readily accommodated, as there is no longer the vested interest of individual application programs to be overcome.

It is important to differentiate between these data management and processing facilities and what are known as 'software application packages'. The application package looks at a business process, payroll perhaps, and the programmers try to write a payroll program that can be used for all payrolls. Inevitably the perfect program cannot be economically constructed, and so in applying an application package the user often finds that he has to make some compromises in his operation to match the way the package is designed.

46

The application package assumes that one payroll is sufficiently similar to another for a general solution to be adopted. The data management and processing facilities on the other hand aim to provide a program module for each processing function; thus the user is able to select those modules which process the data in the way he wants it processed, rather than be forced to change the way he wants to process the data to match the application package.

Future developments in processing

In this book, so far, two fundamentals have been presented: first there was the nature of the data and the meaning of the data base, and second the fundamentals of processing. These two are now linked together to indicate the direction of current developments in data-processing techniques.

The data base provides a common reliable source of data made viable by its involvement with day-to-day operations—available not only to serve those operations but also as a source for management information to draw on. An important ingredient necessary for the data base is flexibility and the ability to react to change; thus management of the data must minimize the impact of change.

This can be achieved by allowing applications using data to be developed independently of the way in which the data is organized. This is possible with the help of data-base management techniques which allow the data to be used without requiring the user to know directly the current physical location of the data within the data base. As long as the user correctly describes the data, data-base management techniques will make that data available to the user's system.

As previously indicated, the processing requirements of any application can be met with these facilities which are made specific to each individual application by providing them with parameters describing the data to be used in the processing; but because these facilities are used through the data-base management system, it is not necessary for the user to give the location of the data. The reactions to new situations therefore are automatically catered for within the data base, and only require the selection of the necessary utility programs and the setting of appropriate parameters defining the new selection of data to be dealt with. These utility programs are analogous to a machine tool, with the data parameters performing the function of a jig.

There are developments under way for bringing the computer even nearer the problem.

A satisfactory method of defining a problem by presenting the appearance and contents of the solution is leading us towards the next stage of computer data processing. Given a suitable problem-statement language, the person with the problem can present it to the computer by describing the data elements he needs to examine and the reports he wishes to be produced from them. The computer can then assemble the optimum selection of processing facilities needed to compose the solution, can refer to the data management system for the current location of the relevant data elements, and present the original inquirer with the solution he is seeking without the intervention of either system analysts or programmers. This surely will bring home to the users that the problems and the solutions are in their hands; and whereas now they hesitate to use the human intermediaries who provide the technical link between them and the computer, and shy away from the computer, a problem-statement language would truly bring the computer into perspective in its role as their working tool for problem solving. Such a language, using normal English terms, allows the user to express his problem, to state the data required for its resolution and the nature of the end product. His statements are then submitted for running on the computer and the user is supplied with the output he specified.

Identification and coding

An important ingredient of successful processing is the positive identification of the things to be processed and their status. The identification usually takes one of three forms: first it can be a precise description in plain English; second it may be an alpha/numerical code containing logic which acts as a form of description; or thirdly a unique alpha/numerical code containing no descriptive or logical aspects but bearing a reference which leads to this description. In the first two cases the identification usually contains generic as well as specific information, so the problem of grouping at various levels is solved by selecting the appropriate generic element of the identifier; of course the greater the number of generic levels required, the longer the identifier becomes.

Before there were any mechanical aids to processing, the precise description provided the only practical means of identification; the voluminous army catalogues bear witness to this, and also demonstrate the tortuousness of combining both precise and generic information in the one identifier: 'boots, feet, men for the use of'.

This identification is necessary not only for the specific item under review, but also the various states or conditions through which the item passes. It is of course not only concerned with item identification

48

but also with such things as location codes and account head codes.

The great advantage of this descriptive system is that all those who come in contact with a reference to this identifier have a greater chance of understanding it. However, this very ease of understanding creates problems of precision, as different people interpret the same words in different ways. It is not only the individual item that causes difficulties: the generic identification can prove most misleading. Take as an example the word 'stocks'. In many operations 'stocks' play an important part, and identification and description of these stocks is necessary not only for the day-to-day operational requirements, but also to meet the accounting needs. But what are stocks? To the manufacturer the description 'stocks' encompasses his raw materials or stock of bought-out items; the capital tied up in the process starting with the acquisition of these stocks and ending with a finished product is usually referred to as 'stock and work in progress'. However, within the same organization there are other sorts of stocks; there is for example the stock of completed products. To the administrative department, stocks may even refer to the stationery store. If one restricts oneself to stocks of finished products, there still remain problems of precision. When does an item start and stop being a stock item? There are often 'pipeline' stocks linking completed items with the manufacturing process at one end, and the ultimate destination at the other. Also stocks may be held in a number of locations. Sometimes there will be some significance in the location and at other times the locations result from haphazard or arbitrary circumstances; thus the identification of the location in those cases where specific categories are stored in specific locations has far more meaning than identification of the location in the other cases. In the case of a heavy electrical manufacturer, a study was undertaken into the various categories of 'stocks' of completed products. In all, ninety-seven categories were identified! Common usage often results in certain categories being identified in a jargon that is meaningless except to those completely familiar with its usage, and thus yet another 'business language' is developed.

Words, because of their ambiguity, probably provide the least satisfactory way of identifying items or status. The difficulty of being precise when communicating with words was well illustrated by the precise and specialist language that had to be developed for the Apollo space projects to enable the men in mission control at base and the men in the space vehicle to talk to each other about such straightforward activities as eating and sleeping. (I am reminded of the Englishman with a heavy cold staying in a Paris hotel. In his best French he asked for a 'Vin

49

chaud' and a few minutes later was informed that his 'bain chaud' was ready!)

The final difficulty with words to examine is that as soon as one considers mechanical processing techniques, the processing of alphabetical descriptions becomes difficult and cumbersome, thus the mechanical functions of processing provide further restrictions on the shape of the description: how many characters can be used? what is the significance of the position of each word in the description? Consider the havoc that can be caused in mechanical processing by a simple spelling mistake, or the presence or absence of a full-stop.

The second form of identifier is the alpha/numeric logical code which places the item being identified within a logical framework. Anyone reading one of the codes can glean a lot of information about the item without seeking out any reference document which will provide the precise definition of the item. There is always in the background this reference document or code book, nearly always manually prepared, which gives a precise and detailed description for every code. When good discipline is associated with the preparation and updating of this code book, this type of identification is very valuable and is probably that most in use.

The crucial stage in this system is the allocation of the code in the first place, as all future processing, analysing and grouping will be directly influenced by that code. However, there are two dangers that need to be avoided. The first is to ensure that the codes are intelligently used: it is all too easy to relegate the routine task of 'coding' to a group of junior employees, but the intelligence with which they apply the codes can have a profound effect upon the ability of the organization to find out about itself. It is unlikely that the coding clerk will have much knowledge of the processing requirements, and yet the process of coding is essentially a discretionary one requiring him to interpret some written description into the coding structure. The second danger is related to the first in that it arises out of the coding need, and that is that the existence of a logical coding structure acts as a fog which masks any new situations that arise. There is a strong tendency to force things into conforming to the existing codes, or perhaps to allocate them to a 'miscellaneous' or 'other' category.

In a steady or slowly changing situation the logical code provides the most useful way of identifying items or status for processing purposes: not only does it present a ready-made logic to the processing but through familiarity and its descriptive element it is also easy to handle by the clerical workers. However, it does resist change. The logical coding structure, by the very presence of its inbuilt logic, gives the system a lethargy of vested interest against change. A re-grouping or the expression of a re-organization may require a complete restructuring of the code, and until this happens the processing is not able to reflect the real world.

Here is an example concerned with location or organization codes: the sub-division of the U.K. into sales territories.

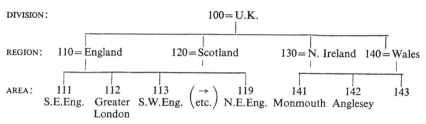

DIVISION: 100=U.K.

REGION: 110=England   120=Scotland   130=N. Ireland 140=Wales

AREA: 111   112   113   (→)   119   141   142   143
     S.E.Eng. Greater S.W.Eng. (etc.) N.E.Eng. Monmouth Anglesey
               London

In the more active sales areas there may be say 150 salesmen each generating paper work which records sales activities, orders placed, customer comments, and so forth. At any one time a substantial pipeline of this paper work exists and also numerous files, each containing information coded with the area, regional and divisional code. Then a change comes along! This could be of two sorts. The first might be the sub-division of an existing area, Greater London into 'North of the Thames' and 'South of the Thames', for example. The second might be the reallocation of areas to different regions: Monmouth to be serviced by Region 110 perhaps. In both cases the code has a built-in resistance to these changes. If one examines the England areas it is apparent that the codes 111-119 are all used up; how does one now accommodate another area? Extend to a four-digit code? This may sound simple to the sales management who, if administrative discipline is loose, may proceed to do this, but it causes chaos in the processing and analytical functions. Even if another suitable code can be found— let us say 118 has not been in use for the last six months or so and we can therefore re-code Monmouth from 141 to 118—a different chaos ensues whilst all outstanding records are changed, and the pipeline of paperwork is processed, and all those who generate paper-work are re-educated.

This is obviously a simple and isolated example, but in any substantial organization having coding structures which isolate comparatively low levels of activity, these situations are occurring all the time, and because it becomes increasingly difficult for the logical coding structure to be kept up to date, so the ability to report on and analyse

51

INTERNATIONAL INGESTOR CORPORATION LIMITED
SUMMARY OF MACHINE ORDERS† CANCELLATIONS AND WITHDRAWALS

PERIOD 13 ENDED 28.09.69   YEAR TO DATE

VALUES IN TERMS OF £'000's OF NOTIONAL WORKS COST

		DIRECT SALES				OTHER SALES	
		Retail Outlets	Customer	Wholesale	Grand Total	Own Use	Dealers
INGESTORS	20-PHASE	34 47·1%	—	38 52·9%	72 100·0% (a)	—	— 0·1%	— 0·3%
INGESTORS	40-PHASE	447 30·3%	—	1027 69·7%	1475 100·0%	—	−27 −1·8%	87 5·5%
INGESTORS	65-PHASE	18 21·8%	—	63 78·2%	87 100·0% (a)	—	3 3·5%	—
INGESTORS	80-PHASE	2093 23·9%	4 *	6671 76·1%	8767 100·0% (b)	—	330 3·4%	531 5·7%
MULTI-STAGE INGESTORS		20 14·9%	—	114 85·1%	134 100·0% (a)	—	— −0·3%	10 7·0%
HYPER-INGESTORS‡		5773 60·5%	—	3764 39·5%	9537 100·0% (b)	—	45 0·4%	783 7·6%
SALES TO TRADE		262 100·0%	—	—	262 100·0% (a)	—	4 1·5%	—
GRAND TOTAL		8647 42·5%	4 *	11677 57·4%	20327 100·0%	—	354 1·6%	1411 6·5%

* Denotes non-significance

† Excluding own use machines, and including orders to be met from local overseas sources.
‡ Includes 13-phase Ingestors.

(a) These four items only account for under 3% of the total.
(b) These two items account for 90% of the total.

Fig. 3.1: A return becoming increasingly irrelevant because of an obsolete code structure.

the organization's activity in any useful way is reduced. Fig. 3.1 illustrates a return which suffered from this problem. Because of a change in the business patterns, although there is a matrix of figures on the return, virtually 50% of the value falls on one figure only and the values for the other figures are minimal.

Two coding systems have been illustrated so far. The first is a discipline code where words, or abbreviations, are used throughout and it is easy to interpret the codes but not very easy to perform mechanical, analytical work on them. The second is a logical code where numbers or letters are used in a structured way to identify things, and the logic of this structure makes the process of analysing and reporting a straightforward one. Both these systems represent obstacles to change as they foster an in-built interest for retaining the *status quo*.

The arrival of high-speed processing makes it possible to exploit other techniques, in particular the allocation of unique codes. Before describing the principles of unique coding structure, the processing technique which makes it possible will be illustrated with a brief case study, which might be entitled 'The after-merger inventory'.

A perplexing problem arose when examining the difficulty of controlling the inventory of spare parts in a manufacturing organization that had undergone a number of mergers. The mergers brought manufacturers of like products together and out of the commonality of their activity it was possible to bring about a substantial rationalization. The control of all the spares, for example, was placed in the hands of a store controller who was responsible for the holdings in the base store and in a number of subsidiary depots.

On studying the inventory activity a puzzling situation emerged. A storeman would go to a bin in response to a demand, and finding the bin empty, would then, through the appropriate channels, place an order on the factory and record the demand in the 'dues out' file. The puzzle was that the parts never arrived in the store from the factory, although the factory claimed to have satisfied the order. This type of situation kept occurring; the dues out increased, relations between the stores and the factory deteriorated, and the whole activity became very inefficient. At the same time, in another part of the base store, parts kept arriving, bins were overflowing and supply greatly exceeded demand.

As soon as one relates these two situations, the answer becomes clear: the same part but different part numbers! However, with a merger store carrying, say, 150,000 different parts numbers and processing several thousand transactions a day, this situation is not readily isolated. In this particular example, 14,000 parts were identified with more than one part number, many of them with up to seven part numbers and even one part known under thirteen part numbers. Such situations arise not only as a result of mergers. For example, it may be decided to manufacture in house a part previously bought from three different suppliers; thus in addition to the three existing part numbers, one given by each outside supplier, there will now be a fourth, the in-house manufacturing number. It is pure chance whether the demand for that part uses the same number under which there happens to be stock available.

What is the answer? Renumber all the parts? This would entail not only renumbering the 150,000 parts, but reissuing all the parts manuals in use all over the world! Maybe in some remoter areas equipment is in use which has not been manufactured for twenty years; however, it still needs parts, and the bible is the parts manual supplied when the equipment was originally delivered. It would not only be a question of renumbering all the parts, but also of ensuring that the new manuals got into the hands of the right people. In a tightly controlled situation, such as the armed forces, this might be possible, but when the person indenting for parts is in no way controlled by the person supplying the parts (the opposite in fact: he may be a customer whose goodwill has to be protected), a comprehensive renumbering is extremely difficult, if not impossible.

The solution to the particular situation used as an example here was to cocoon the inventory control system in a 'Common Part Number Index'. The order and demand processing was computerized, but before any external event was actioned within the inventory system it was subjected to the computer-held common part number index. This was simply a statement of all identified multiple part numbers, designating one of them to be used as the master number for inventory control, storage and like process. The user is able to indent according to the part number with which he is familiar, this indent is processed through the index and the part number used for storage indentified; the order is then processed using that number, but carrying a tag identifying the number used on the original order so that when the part is subsequently despatched it goes out in a calico bag carrying the number that the user will recognize as the one he asked for.

This particular situation illustrates the ability of a computer system to create order out of an apparently disorganized or haphazard external situation, and it is this ability that can be exploited to provide an infinitely flexible coding structure that presents no obstacle to change.

54

The principle of the third type, the unique coding system, is that the code contains no in-built logic; instead it is just a number that is unique to the particular thing it is identifying. When a new situation or item needs identifying the next free number in the sequence is allocated, and these numbers bear no logical relationship one to another. The logic is contained in a conversion table held on the computer; in the same way that the common part number index created order out of external disorder, so a conversion table can give a structure to a collection of unique numbers. Not only that, but the structure can be added to, reorganized or changed without difficulty by simply feeding a new conversion table into the computer.

No system, however, is without its own problems. The difficulty with a unique coding system is the very ease with which new codes can be allocated; it can be much easier to allocate a new code than think whether the new code is really necessary. However, with central control over the allocation of these codes it is possible to effect this discipline without too great an administrative overhead.

This chapter has described three methods of 'identification'. This has been to demonstrate the fundamental importance of the subject if one is going to create a processing system which can truly serve, and which can react to all the changes that are going to be required of it rather than stand as an impediment to change.

Chapter 4

People and the Computer

Man and his mind

'To place any discussions of problems in their proper perspective, we should recognize that a total system is the integration of technology with people, procedures and facilities, which is another way of saying that we need to consider technology as it relates to the operational environment. There has been much preoccupation with technology for its own sake, with the not too surprising result that technological success has often been accompanied by failure to provide the user with a useful system. . . . We have an adequate technology base, although there are unsolved problems which are potential areas of improvement. We are not really constrained by technology. Our hardware and software choices are extensive, with an accompanying wide range of costs. But we need to concentrate more on the systems' externals, that is to say, on the people and the operational environment in which they function. I don't believe that the technological problems still facing us can be used as an excuse for failing to implement effective, or, said differently, useful systems; and the user is becoming increasingly aware of this'.[1]

The common denominator between the horseless carriage and a computerized payroll is the limitations imposed by the human brain, and we have far too little understanding of these limitations. Two characteristics of mental activity illustrate the point.

The first of these is the satisfaction that comes from abstract intellectual activity. This appears in a multitude of forms but they all have the one feature of being cut off from life.

[1] *Information Management Systems, State-of-the-Art,* by Ben Erdman of the U.S. Defence Communications Agency and member of a panel set up by The Fall Joint Computer Conference to report on information management systems for the 1970s.

Mathematical progressions, the pursuit of the classics, music in its purer form, all offer fascinating opportunities for mental detachment. The relentless development of the logic of an idea in whatever field offers continual and almost irresistible temptation to the brain. There is a certain sort of programmer who can never complete a program! He can always find one more twist to the logic, one more sub-routine to develop.

The second characteristic is by way of a mirror image of the first. It is a shying away from thinking about those situations that do not lend themselves to the exercise of intellectual logic. It is very difficult to quantify or explore logically the mathematical values of human reaction or interaction. The works manager may well know that the potential output from his workshop over the next week will be reduced because the foreman's wife has just run away from him and he is taking it out on his men, but the mathematical model can never know this. Anyway, the mathematical value of one man's wife running away from him would be quite different from that in the case of another man.

It is very difficult for the scientist when faced with problems, business or organizational, to avoid the temptations of the wholly logical solution. Where the problem is predominantly technical, such as landing a man on the moon, the scientist can achieve considerable success, but where his solution has to be applied by men in an environment of other men, the success is very much more dependent upon these men than upon scientific logic.

It is perhaps overstating the case to argue that programming is now providing the emotional escape that previous generations found in theoretical theology or study of the classics—with those who cannot face up to the realities of the emotional world of human relationship finding solace in elegant programming. However, the danger does exist and must be recognized!

It is with this background that we are attempting to inject science into the provision of information given to a manager who has to take a decision, and the moral to be drawn is that our solution cannot successfully be wholly scientific. We must so construct an information system that people can influence the nature and controls on the input, can choose parameters for the processing, and most important of all, can interpret, understand and use the output.

Computers for management decisions

In what way can the resources of computing contribute to management decisions?

Firstly, a virtually unlimited volume of data can be received and stored. Computing alone cannot control this data; it can only exercise the controls that people establish.

Next, this data can be processed and innumerable calculations undertaken at fantastic speeds. Of course innumerable errors can be compounded if people have not correctly defined these calculations.

Finally, data and information can be made available, transmitted and presented in a variety of ways and over great distances. The relevance of the data or information to the person to whom it is presented, however, depends upon the people who define it. If someone dies from electric shock, one does not blame the electricity but the people who arranged the system to use electricity in such a way as to expose people to the danger of shock. Similarly, if someone drowns under a deluge of paper, one does not blame the computing but the people who arranged the systems in such a way as to produce the deluge.

Let us take each of these categories of activity and examine its potential contribution to management decisions.

Data does not belong to a department or a section, it belongs to the whole organization. A particular department or section may be a prime user of that data and confidentiality or the delegated organization structures may restrict access to it, but data is a crucial asset of the organization. I have shown how, by exercising the proper disciplines and controls over the data within an organization, one can create a data base which contains *reliable*, unambiguous data about what is going on within that organization. This reliable source of data becomes a foundation upon which decisions can be built. To *know* such things as what there is in stock, the state of the order book, how many employees there are, and to have confidence in this information, reduces the element of guess in making the decision and increases the element of fact.

Of course a data base is not a computer! It certainly must not be confused with a vast random-access file in the centre of the organization; this would be rather like confusing a journey with a motor car! I have defined a data base as the logical organization of the data within an organization, with a master updating location for each element of data.

However, a data base is not something that just happens! To be successful it requires that for every element of data there must be a line manager who understands and accepts the responsibility for updating it.

Data permeates the whole organization: it is no respecter of human or organizational boundaries and, as already said, it belongs to the whole organization. It follows that the founding of a data base can only result from a deliberate act of corporate policy. However, given that initiative, the contribution of a well-ordered data base to the efficiency of an organization is enormous.

The processing of data and the calculations that computing power make possible can contribute to management decisions in two ways.

First, the data in the data base can be combined, grouped and related together, so as to provide a formal reporting structure, a flow of information to form the backbone for the organization. Historically, this has only happened with financial information, and often only in an imperfect way. Data is more fundamental than financial information; data provides the elements for the information molecules, so to speak— financial information is certainly a class of molecule but there are many others. The formal reporting structure makes available to the decision-maker reliable information of the sort already mentioned: stocks, orders, personnel, and so forth. Also a management decision to change the formal reporting structure can be rapidly and precisely implemented —as long as it is precisely defined.

Secondly, the ability to undertake innumerable rapid calculations opens up a whole new world to the decision process, and as with all new worlds the rewards are matched by the dangers! This is the world of modelling and simulation. These techniques are not new in themselves: most of us use simple models on a day-to-day basis. Take, for example, a transport manager with 50 tons to move and a fleet of 5-ton trucks; he uses his 'model' to decide how many trucks to use and how many journeys to make. The actuary, the statistician and the accountants have all been using models for a long time, but without access to computing power any one series of calculations represented a long and laborious process.

Computing power has brought about a number of changes. It makes it possible to process a model using a particular set of values, observe the result, change the values, observe the result, change the values again, and so on. All this can be done rapidly; thus it now becomes possible to explore the implementing of a whole range of alternative courses of action.

In addition, much more complex models can now be readily processed; although many people do not favour these, and prefer simple models or a number of individual models exploring different but related aspects of the total business.

Finally, and perhaps most important, these models are becoming increasingly easy to develop and use. Their bias is moving away from the technician towards the manager, and as managers gain confidence in their ability to grapple with these techniques, they can make increasing use of them without having to acquire technical expertise.

Thus a manager is now able to test alternative decisions before actually committing himself to any particular one. Perhaps this is a bit too glib. Right at the start it was said that non-formal information, intuition and judgement all contribute to a management decision. Modelling techniques make it possible to limit these non-quantifiable attributes so that when they are essential they receive the attention they deserve; this is because that which is quantifiable has been reliably reported and its implications accurately tested. To be of value information must be readily available; it must be possible to refine from a not-too-precise need for information to a precise answer. At the same time there is a danger in the information being too readily available. If organizational delegation is to have any meaning, the more senior the manager, the more it is necessary for the information he receives to be interpreted by the executive responsible for the functions in question. By whom should the information be presented? Computing power can be used in a variety of ways to present information, as in computer print-out, microfilm, visual display units, graph plotters, teletypes; but the information that is presented must have a source. If it represents data in the data base that has been processed, someone must have decided in what way it should be processed.

The danger is that a team of people may emerge in the centre of the organization who generate information or design systems to process data to present information to the senior management, without any reference to the manager of the function to which the information refers.

Any confidence the senior management might have in the computer will be rapidly eroded by the caustic comments of these line managers, who will view the information as a form of snooping and try energetically to discredit it. As with data, information is a line management responsibility. The proper man to underwrite information about the value of invoices sent out this month is the man responsible for sending out the invoices! It follows that as well as a corporate data policy, it is necessary to consider a corporate information policy—what information, from whom, according to what standards, reflectings what controls, supporting what organization structure.

Systems development

In developing any system, but particularly a computer-based management information system, whilst success depends to some extent upon the technical expertise involved in its development and the sophistication of the facilities provided, it depends much more upon the extent to which the people for whom it is developed understand and use it. There are too many systems based upon magnificent and foolproof theory which fall flat on their face because of this lack of understanding.

Management understanding comes not from academic learning but from the experience that arises out of practical doing. This subject will be dealt with later, but at this point it is necessary only to emphasize that to be successful the ultimate user of a system must become involved with the development of that system so that he, as well as those technicians concerned with its development, can go through the thought processes associated with tackling the problems that arise, and learn about the system by so doing. There is much talk about user education, but there is no education so efficacious as making the user think through the problems himself.

The benefit open to the user by this involvement has been dealt with in some detail, but there is, of course, another benefit—to the system itself. Competent analysis will establish the pattern of the present situation and design the framework for the system to be developed, but only the user knows the absolute detail of all the oddities which are so easily overlooked, and the user is also the person most likely to have a feel for what will really work, as opposed to what looks nice on paper.

As indicated, the success of a system depends upon the satisfactory interaction between the users and the analysts during its development but, like so many theories, this is not necessarily easy to achieve!

The first thing to realize is that there is rarely just one user. In any operation a whole host of people are involved at all levels, from senior management to junior clerk, and the generic term 'user' encompasses all of these. The man at the top may have the responsibility, but success depends upon understanding by all his staff who are going to be concerned with its operation, and it is all these users who need to get involved with the development.

With such a range of staff concerned, each with his own parochial interest, it is clearly not adequate merely to form a 'project steering group' where all interested parties sit round a table once a month, drink endless cups of coffee, have wonderful disagreements, and at the end of two years decide to form an old boys' club. User involvement is much more complex than that, but rather than generalize upon its nature, a specific structure is here presented to illustrate the general situation.

In any major development there are at least three levels of involvement: first there is the senior management policy level; second the technical systems steering level; and third the individual problem project level. The first level guides the development by establishing the policy framework within which it should operate and resolving any significant organizational problems that arise. Frequent meetings are not usually necessary, although at formative stages this group will meet more frequently than when the hard grind of the detailed development is under way. It is essential to retain a degree of flexibility in their frequency to ensure that the meetings arise out of necessity rather than out of habit. The chairman is the senior line executive responsible; appropriate members of his senior staff attend as nominated by him for particular meetings, and of course the senior systems staff who also provide the secretariat.

Very often the man at the top will attempt to delegate the responsibility for the project to his 'computerization officer'. However, this delegation is often a symptom of his fear and lack of understanding of the project. Although one must not overtly thwart this delegation (in fact it can be put to good use), it is essential that the person who is really going to carry the responsibility for the project should be involved in its development by chairing the policy group.

The second level is the one which exploits this delegation to a 'computerization officer', as this level acts as the co-ordination forum for the project. Here the meetings take place more regularly, and all those concerned with the development know that they can refer any particular problem they are unable to resolve to its next meeting. This group will call for reports and monitor progress on each aspect of the project. It is useful here also to have the users' representative in the chair if there is a logical one person who can do this. More often, however, there are three or four senior people directly concerned and to nominate one of them as chairman increases the interdepartmental friction and rivalries. Two alternatives exist: either the chairmanship goes by rota or the senior systems man acts as chairman. Rivalries, however, often create a serious problem, as a frequent aspect of advanced computer systems is that they break down the demarcation between existing organizational units, and so it is usually more satisfactory in these circumstances for the senior systems man to act as chairman. He can then exercise all his tact, training and experience in trying to get all the warring parties to act as a team, but he knows that he can refer serious problems that arise to the policy group, if necessary stimulating a special *ad hoc* meeting of this group.

The third level of involvement is in many ways the most important— the involvement of the staff who are actually doing the job. It is involvement at the working level by those people who are going to have to work the new system. Their understanding of their part in it, and the relationship their operation holds to the total system are what ultimately matter. Managers may come and go, but the work goes on. . . !

Many individuals will be affected by, or are concerned with, operating a system—clerks, supervisors, data-preparing staff, and many others—and it is the involvement of these people in the development phase that is so crucial.

As individual problems are isolated in the development it is possible to establish a project team to work on their solution, and to draw the staff for these project teams primarily from those who have experience on the job. Such project teams would normally have quite a short life, up to six weeks perhaps, during which time they may only meet perhaps four or five times, and they would have very precise terms of reference. One project team will often generate another by isolating further problems, and because all the significant operational staff work on one or more of these project teams, one can have some confidence that all the operational situations and problems that are likely to arise will have been exposed.

In general, a member of the systems staff would be included in the project team, usually as the leader or secretary, but this is not an invariable rule as long as the systems staff provide the co-ordination between one project team and another.

One could argue that the existence of these project teams delays the ultimate development of the system, especially as the number of project teams involved in a major system can run into three figures, and it is certainly quite true that this work does slow down the development of a theoretical solution. However, the objective of a systems development is not a theoretical solution but a practical solution which will work! These project teams greatly speed the eventual achievement of that particular objective.

In addition to the three levels of involvement there is a fourth level, right at the top, which gives expression to company policies. One way in which it can direct the policy is to fund all systems development from a systems development fund administered by this top group. All major projects have to be justified to them and they ensure that company policies are reflected by the way in which they distribute this central systems development fund.

One should be cautious about establishing too rigid a structure for organizing the effort concerned with the development of a system. One should certainly have a general framework but one should be quite

63

prepared to modify it according to any particular set of circumstances. In particular it is necessary to isolate those people in the existing operation who really matter and ensure that they are able to contribute to the full. The senior members of staff rarely know in any degree of detail what goes on or what day-to-day problems occur; yet it is all too easy to develop a system in accordance with the understanding these senior people have of their job, only to find it founders on these day-to-day problems. However, it is usually difficult to arrange for the more junior staff to have time off to join in the activities of the project teams, because the current operation of the company has come to depend so much upon them.

Nonetheless, their participation is vital and some means has to be found to make them available. For this reason the selection of the users' staff who are going to be concerned with the development at all levels is not always something that can be left to the user. He will often be inclined to exclude his key people from participating because they are too busy and too much concerned with keeping the current operation going.

A particular structure of user involvement in the development of a system has been outlined as the policy level, the technical level, and the working level. If this involvement has been successfully achieved, then the system that is developed will work. It will work because those who have real experience in the problem have helped to develop the solution, because those who are going to have to operate the system have become involved with its development and so have gained an insight into what it is all about, but predominantly it will work because those who are going to use the new system will feel a personal responsibility towards it.

Who is responsible?

Management scientist and systems staff are concerned with working with a user to develop a solution to his problems. They may well exert considerable influence over the nature of the solution, particularly where an overall pattern has been developed, as it has to be if one is incorporating the principles of the data base and building up towards a management information system. Nonetheless, the systems staff do not operate the systems they develop; the user does that. Similarly, the computer staff are responsible for providing a resource: computing power. They are concerned to ensure that it is an efficient resource, and that the data provided by the user is correctly reflected in what comes out and is in accordance with the controls established for the system. They operate the computer but they are not responsible for operating the system, this responsibility falls squarely on the user. Two aspects of this user responsibility need exploring: his responsibility first, towards the operation of the system itself; and, secondly, towards the data used by the system.

To over-simplify the position: there are four levels of people concerned with a system. There are those whom the system is ultimately designed to serve (in a payroll system this would be the people who are paid), there are those who use the system (the payroll staff); there are those who work on the development of the system; and there are those who provide the computing resource.

Taking the example of a payroll makes the demarcation between 'who is responsible for what' fairly straightforward (although this will become confused in discussing responsibility for data) because historically there had always been a strong, well-controlled payroll operation and few paymasters would permit the complete control of the operation of the payroll to pass from them. In fact this inclination for complete control often causes them to encroach on other areas of responsibility—the operation of the computer, for example. However, there are many activities less precise than the payroll where the responsibility for operating the system is less clearly defined. This is particularly the case if the system introduces a new grouping of responsibilities so that the previous pattern of who is responsible for what is no longer valid. In these situations it is all too easy for the systems and computer operations staff to slide into the position of running the system, with the normal management only dimly aware of what goes on.

One of the problems is that, as the ultimate recipient is usually aware that what he is receiving is generated from the computer, he has a tendency to blame the computer for anything that goes wrong. It is all too easy to telephone the computer manager and curse him for that computer of his, when the real problem lies in the operation of the system by the user. Unfortunately, the user will often promote this idea by hiding behind the computer if anything goes wrong, transferring the blame from himself, where it truly belongs, to the computer.

In this way 'the computer' is rapidly becoming one of society's overworked scapegoats, blamed for all the social evils and quite unable to defend itself. The computer is not a super-brain; it cannot with Machiavellian intent usurp the powers that should properly be exercised by society. It is quiet, thorough and efficient, and it does what it is told, exactly what it is told, every time, without deviation. The people with the responsibility are the people who tell it what to do, the users, and we must not let them blame the computer for what is their fault. If a non-

65

sense electricity bill is sent out, the fault does not lie with the computer, which received data and processed it in the exact way in which it was instructed. Someone, some person, some human being, somewhere along the line has made a mistake. It is that person, and the chain of command above him, who are responsible, and it is therefore necessary to seek out that person and make sure he does not make the same mistake again. Let us hear no more of this 'I'm sorry, our computer made a mistake'!

The tarnished public image of computers results from the ease with which people can avoid responsibility by putting the blame on the computer. In the operation of any system, the user is responsible. He is responsible for seeing that what goes in is right, and for ensuring that the system is so designed that what comes out correctly reflects what goes in.

A properly maintained car is not blamed for an accident: the driver is held responsible. The car obeys his instructions and if, as a result of his instructions being wrong or too slow, an accident occurs, the driver is taken to court, not the car. He cannot say, 'I'm sorry, my car made a mistake'. There has to be a proper chain of command and delegation of authority, but this authority must never be delegated to the computer or to those staff directly responsible for running it; the user, not the computer, is responsible for the system.

A further aspect of user responsibility lies at the precise working level of each element of data. It is quite essential that there should be absolutely unambiguous responsibility for each data element. This is particularly the case with a data base system as each data element has only one master updating location; it is clearly necessary to establish who has the responsibility for this updating.

In earlier application-oriented data files the problem was not so acute. Each system had its own data file and the user of that system updated the data elements in that data file. As shown earlier in this book, the result was that the same data elements would appear in a number of files but at least there was a clear responsibility for each entry. With the data base, only one stream of updating is possible for each data element, and it is essential for that updating stream to satisfy all the systems using the element.

Where the data element is of a precise, factual nature, the main problem is how to trap it at source and who should be responsible for this. As already shown, there are other sorts of data, either qualitative in nature, or not lending themselves to precise quantitative control, where the problem is rather more difficult.

66

With the precise elements one can identify three general situations. First there are those cases where an element has a prime user and it is easy to get the other users of the element to acknowledge this. Thus the prime user becomes responsible for the updating and the system will work efficiently. The second situation is where there are a number of users but no one clearly dominates, and they all have slightly different interests, perhaps reflected in the different frequency of updating. In these cases it is possible for one of them to be nominated as a prime user and his terms of reference widened to cope with the other interests, but there is always the danger that he will bias the updating towards his particular use. It may be more satisfactory to establish a non-parochial data control function to deal with these situations, as long as the allocation of responsibility for updating a data element to the data control unit is regarded as a last resort rather than the first recourse. However, there are always certain key elements that are so vital to the operation of a wide range of systems that non-parochial control is essential. An example of this category might be the receiving of names and addresses of customers under query, deciding if they are new customers and, if so, allocating them a customer number; and, if not, establishing which existing customer number should be used. If XYZ Ltd represents a customer to the data base in question, there may well be a large number of locations identified in the data base with different customer numbers all under the general heading of XYZ. The data control function having allocated a customer number to be used for say 'XYZ Ltd, Pontypool', may be faced with the problem of deciding whether the same number should be used for a piece of paper quoting 'The Exwyzed Company Limited (South Wales)'. Customer numbers will be used in such a variety of systems that it is essential these are all considered when allocating and controlling the numbers and resolving these sorts of difficulties.

The third situation with precise data elements is where, though there is an apparent prime user, he is not the proper person who should have the responsibility for updating the data element. The payroll provides a very good example of this. Although the prime user of payroll data, annual salary and so forth, is the pay office, the responsibility for updating this data lies outside the pay office. In the case study of the personnel data base detailed in Chapter 2, we saw how the responsibility rests with the personnel office working on information provided by the managers. The personnel authorities are concerned with negotiating wage and salary scales, with hiring and firing, and with interpretation of the organization remuneration policy, and it is therefore they who have the responsibility for saying how much a person should be paid, also what is his correct name, his address, and so forth. The pay office has a responsibility for updating certain data elements associated with the payroll, tax code for example, but in general the payroll systems use elements in the data base that are provided by and are the responsibility of the personnel office. The pay office is clearly responsible for the system that manipulates these elements and as a result produces a pay slip or wage packet, and also for providing those data elements that clearly do belong to it, but they do not have the responsibility for the bulk of the data they use.

The example taken from the payroll will readily suggest the sort of political and emotional problems that emerge when one pursues the data base concept. The resolution of problems such as these is a great help in defining the responsibility people have towards the systems they use, and the data-base elements these systems require.

There is a great tendency to discount the political and emotional problems but, in all but the most abstract application, success depends upon people, individual understanding, and the interactions between people. Introduction of a data base results in many changes to individual daily routines and responsibilities; in practice these changes might be quite small but anticipation of them can create substantial obstacles to progress. Similarly a person's power and authority often derive from the knowledge and data to which only he has access; to make this publicly available can appear to detract from his prestige; it also exposes to the critical world the imperfections of the data which he currently uses.

When establishing the routines for updating the data base it is necessary to identify the prime user for each element of data. Once identified, many weeks of persuasion and political negotiations are necessary before the new distribution of responsibilities can operate effectively. Nor is it wise to force a particular issue, for, like a complex piece of machinery, an organization depends not upon individual actions but the interaction of individual actions.

Those data elements that do not lend themselves to precise control present rather a different sort of situation. There is the question of who is going to be responsible for them and how they are going to be updated; but there is also the question of how they are going to be used— which is related to the problem of their continuing validity.

Those who control a data base are often approached with requests to include this category of data in the data base. The existence of something calling itself a management information system leads people to believe that all information is available on every subject and that all they have to do is to ask for it! Suggest to a manager, or worse to a planner, that he should provide you with a list of all the information he would like, and all sorts of wonderful ideas emerge. Take steps to provide all they would like and you will be caught in a quicksand of data from which there is no escape. Suffocation is inevitable. Data can only be recorded in the data base and provided to a user if someone is prepared to accept full responsibility for each data element. A market planner may well wish to relate fluctuating sales to the weather conditions but unless he is prepared to define precisely what he means by 'weather conditions' and accept full financial responsibility for providing updating information on a continuing basis, his wish should not be satisfied! It is all too easy to accede to such requests, to devise data systems to make this category of data available, to record and update it for years, only to find that it has only been used once and then discarded because it is not in quite the right form, or the market planner whose idea and enthusiasm created the requirement no longer works for the company. Unless the continuing charge for routine updating of this information appears as a regular item on the user's budget, so that he has to justify it, not only when he wants to use the information, but all the time it has to be updated—unless this is the case, the data should not be included in the data base.

Money is not the only constraint. There remains the problem of who should provide this type of data and who should be responsible for the updating process. Unless there is a well-defined source and authority for the data, and the user is prepared to establish and maintain the rules for its interpretation, the user himself must provide the data he requires.

For example, it would be quite possible for the user to agree with the Meteorological Office a routine and a structure for the provision of data concerned with weather conditions. An updating system to accept this data can be established, and the user is only concerned with financing it and ensuring the continued relevance of the structure. However, the data might be far more ambiguous, and in such cases only the user can decide what data should be recorded. An example of this situation might concern data about competitive activity. Information will be flowing in from the sales force giving details about the competitive situations they are experiencing; at the same time the commercial intelligence unit might be scrutinizing all general and technical publications for information on competitive developments. The salesman might say that this 'prospect' has ordered a competitive 10-phase

Ingestor, whilst the trade press might record an order from that customer for a 20-phase Ingestor; the questions to be answered are, how many ingestors have been ordered, one or two; and if one, is it a 10-phase model or a 20-phase model? The interested party, the user who is going to base his analysis upon this information, is the person who should have the responsibility for resolving these conflicts, and he therefore becomes the person responsible for these elements of data on the data base.

Let us suppose that these Ingestors are all-purpose machines but that technical information is required to support each of their many possible uses. This might well create a requirement for including information on applications in the data base. All the rules already established could be followed, and the information user, accepting full responsibility for updating the data base, conscientiously provides regular updating information. As a result the amount of data grows . . . and grows . . . and grows! Updating is a misleading term to use, as it suggests that data is provided which changes the status of the data already on the file. In this example, however, this does not happen; the updating data adds something to the file. It is always adding something to the file, never taking away, never asking the question, 'I know this was the application they used their Ingestor for three years ago, but are they still using it in this way?'

It is quite crucial in any information application where the information is based on this additive type of data, that some routine is established for questioning the continuing relevance of all the data concerned. There should be a 'downdating' procedure, so to speak, as well as an updating one.

The final comment concerns the use of this qualitative data. The prime user, the person who has accepted responsibility for it, will know all about it, will understand it, and will have given it a set of rules dictated by the way in which he wants to use it. There may well be another user, however, who hears about it and would like to use it. It is all too easy to provide this other user with the information he requests and for him to be grossly misled as a result. The interpretation he puts on the definition might be quite different from that of the prime user; the current validity and the frequency of the updating/downdating are all the responsibility of the prime user, and he is the only one who can advise on how this data should be used. Thus, not only is he responsible for updating the data, but to a large extent he 'owns' it and any other party requiring access to it has to do it through him, with his authority and with the benefit of his knowledge of its interpretation and current status. A data base for a management information system is not a cesspool for every haphazard, unco-ordinated, interesting snippet of information that somebody thinks they might want. It is a disciplined body of controlled elements of data, each the responsibility of a clearly defined updating authority.

Intercommunication

The successful operation of any computer system, but more particularly of a management system using information gained from a data base, requires an interaction between the people using the system and the computer providing the information. An earlier section dealt with aspects of this interaction that arise in the development stage and in the provision of and responsibility for data. This section is more concerned with the interaction that must take place when the system is actually being used, so that the operation exploits to the full the differing skills of the computer and of people.

The computer is very good at following rules. But it is essential to distinguish between the rule and the value which should be associated with it. For example, there will certainly be a rule in any inventory control system establishing the re-order point, and the action to be taken when it is reached, and this rule, with its consequential action, can be satisfactorily written into the system.

The value of the re-order point—it may indicate two weeks' stock remaining, or three, for example—must be set as a result of discretion and must be reviewed as time passes and patterns change. The system can even be designed to indicate when the pattern has changed, in order to suggest that the re-order point needs to be reviewed. It can even propose a new value, but the decision should not be treated as an automatic process. The decision must be taken by someone familiar with the situation, who knows the circumstances surrounding this stock holding and can use his judgement on whether the routine and rules still apply in the particular circumstances. Let us take two simple examples. The rule might base re-ordering on the average consumption rate over the past three months, and so the value given might require the minimum stock to equal two weeks' consumption. The re-ordering system will require an average delay factor between placing the order and new stocks arriving, so that the order can be placed in good time in order to avoid stocks falling below the two-weeks level. In this set of rules, therefore, we have isolated the following:

71

Rule written into the system	*Value given by the person responsible and subject to review*
Minimum stock to be based on consumption rate over	past (3) months
Minimum stock not to fall below	(2) weeks stock
Re-order delay factor (i.e. time between placing an order and replacement arriving)	(1) week

Given this sort of framework, however, the user of the system needs to be critically aware of changes which are affecting or are likely to affect the value he places on the rules, and he needs to be continually conscious of what the current values are.

In a number of systems both the rules and their values are built in. This often happens because the user, when specifying his requirements, by describing what he does says, for example, that he usually allows a delay factor of one week. The analysts carefully reflect this requirement when designing the system. However, instead of identifying the rules and their values as two separate functions, there is a danger they will incorporate both as part of the system (in this example, the delay factor and its value of one week). Clearly what one should do is write the rule into the system but require the user to set the value for that rule. It is a useful educational discipline to require the user to set or confirm the values in some way each time the system is run, in order to jog his memory and make him think about them instead of just taking them for granted.

Clearly the rules themselves must not be set as in concrete, but there is a strong case for varying the rules far less frequently than the values, as it is through the consistency in the rules that one gains experience of the effect of altering the values.

If the rules are altered too frequently it becomes much more difficult to obtain a consistency of action because those operating the system are not given the opportunity to learn about it; the whole activity becomes too discretionary, and if there is any volume to be dealt with, it becomes very difficult to control. Of course, in addition to the value option there can be a rule option allowing the user to adopt another set of rules: re-ordering when the stock reaches the minimum economical re-ordering batch size, for example. But the important point is that the success of the control system depends upon this intercommunication, with the system doing the processing but the user setting the values and choosing the options.

Modelling is based entirely upon this, establishing the rules and examining the effects of various values. Those who work with models are very familiar with this exercise of setting values and choosing options, but, unfortunately, they are often not so familiar with the realities of the situation: they have not got the feel for what is really significant. It is all too easy for what is in fact the key value to be set with very little thought, or for sophisticated calculations to be undertaken on basic assumptions that are wildly wrong. Human beings are weak and fallible, and significant decisions are rarely made in a wholly scientific and objective way. This may not be so if the decisions relate to simple, material things—stock levels, for example—but in a complex situation or one affecting human interactions the decision-makers are open to many temptations. In a sea of uncertainties a decision-maker is tempted to clutch at any straw of pseudo-certainty, and the management scientists provide many such straws. These may be positive, precise, numeric solutions; alternatives that can be rated one against another; clear statements on which the decision-maker can exercise judgement so that in a subtle way he is deflected from the sea of uncertainty of the real world to use his judgement on the pseudo-certainty of the numeric world—thus the quality of the decision no longer relies upon his powers of judgement, but upon the quality of the modelling.

One can rightly argue that the most important point on which he should exercise his judgement is to establish the validity of the model and, as in so many other scientific fields, the user must have a deep involvement in developing the model. However, this orientation creates an unsatisfactory environment for the scientist, who now has to compromise his science both by the limitation in the understanding of the decision-taker and by the ill-defined realities of which he is instinctively aware but which defy quantification.

Thus we have a problem of intercommunication: the manager reacting to the system, and the manager and the management scientist reacting with each other, so that the result benefits from the computer's ability to process, the scientist's ability to analyse, and the manager's ability to use judgement and discretion.

There is another quite different aspect of intercommunication. This is the effect that the output from a computer has on the recipient and his ability to react to it. The capacity of the computer for acting as a scapegoat has been already shown; often the recipient is forced into taking this view because of the nature of the output and his frustration at being unable to cope with it.

The appearance and presentation of information will be considered later, but it is axiomatic that any output should be designed keeping in mind the person who has to use it, and should not depend merely on what is easy for the computer to produce. Simply including a person's name on the output, in particular the person to whom queries should be addressed, goes a long way to removing the image of a soulless, mindless computer generating yards of garbage with no one in control. Instead of boasting 'This piece of paper was produced on our computer, which is the latest and most up-to-date model', the boast should be 'This piece of paper was produced for Mr X. on our computer and he will be very pleased to answer any queries you may have on it'. This really reverts to the topic of the user being responsible for the system. The user must accept the full responsibility for what the system produces and be proud of it!

Not only are there man/machine communication problems, but there are, of course, man/man problems! There are many influences which come to bear in information as it flows around an organization. Information and power react upon each other. The possession of information can be used to achieve power, and a position of power gives control over the creation and dissemination of information.

Influence in a corporate structure is enhanced by the knowledge which is held. By stopping a message at his level, a person increases the strength of his position and reduces that of others who are denied the information, thus increasing the differential of power between the person with the information and those without it.

The control which a person can exercise over the information he receives does not only result from the opportunity he has to stop it from passing further. He can also act as a filter, both downwards and upwards, in deciding to whom the information should be further transmitted, in what form, with what bias, and with what selection from the contents. He may also add information, either additional facts or his own interpretation.

Horizontal flows of information also exist, and the barriers to these horizontal flows, particularly between departments are a major source of bureaucratic waste and inefficiency. These barriers often exist right at the top, being reflected at lower levels; the greater the sense of interdepartmental competition existing or the prestige rivalry between the top men, the more difficult these barriers are to overcome.

In most organizations information passes through a number of levels between the point of origin and the point of ultimate decision. The influences already mentioned, and others such as delays due to negligence or overwork, operate at all these levels, both consciously and unconsciously. Thus the journey of a piece of information around an organization can be hazardous. It is into this arena that the computer-based information system introduces the means for greater discipline in the information flow, but it also provides the opportunity for an even greater concentration of power.

The next chapter examines the subject of management information more closely and explores the role of the computer in this confused context.

Chapter 5

Management Information

What is management information?

Management results from the exercise of judgement in the light of the best information that is available. Judgement is employed to control and to motivate men, to analyse and exploit markets, to make effective and profitable use of resources. All these facets of management can be supported by information, which a manager uses to help him prepare his plans, establish and monitor controls, and ensure that co-ordination exists at all levels. However, he will be fulfilling these functions whether information is available or not, making the best use of what is available, and using his experience and perception to complete the picture. The problems of management increase according to the extent to which reliable information is lacking.

The basic concept of the subject of management information is the need to provide and manage with as much reliable and unambiguous information as is relevant to the manager's activity, thereby increasing the amount of hard fact, and reducing the amount of guesswork.

Much study has been made of techniques for providing management information, but studies of this kind frequently beg the question: What *is* management information?

Because the techniques of providing management information have received so much study, it would be possible for me to produce a definitive analysis of the management information systems available—what they will do, their strengths and weaknesses. I could compare one with another, contrasting their facilities. Users have commented upon their experiences and I could therefore compare the claims of the designers with users' actual experience. All this would be possible, and yet we would be no nearer understanding the nature of management information. For this topic there is no body of learning to lean on. One cannot therefore offer a definitive study of the subject, but instead one can present a number of facets drawn from personal observation and experience, and in so doing can explore aspects of management information to try and give it some reality. Out of this exploration will emerge some of the techniques needed to support its provision.

Let me dispel one illusion from the start. It was shown earlier that the data base was not just a vast random-access store in the centre of an organization, but was much more concerned with the logical organization of the data regardless of how or in what medium it was stored. In the same way a management information system is not just a facility for retrieving at will any individual data element from a vast data base. Information retrieval facilities may in some instances contribute towards the successful operation of a management information system, but that is all. They are not the beginning and end of such a system, although an obsession with speed of access appears to puff up the subject of information retrieval until it becomes confused with the management information itself. The relevance of the information is far more crucial than speed, and there are only a few situations where fast access is a relevant item. One piece of relevant information, carefully and methodically prepared, is worth more than any amount of instantly accessible data. There are, however, operational systems where rapid information-retrieval facilities play a most important role—airline ticket booking systems, stock interrogation, and such like—but I wish to make a clear distinction between a manager who is managing a function, and the staff actually doing the job. Management information is required to serve the manager: it is needed to help him take his decisions.

One can illustrate some different categories of such information by the facts relating to a car crash as they affect the police control headquarters. The first fact is that the crash has taken place. There is nothing that can be done to avert it; it has happened and that is the factual situation with which the police have to cope. It is nonetheless information in that it causes them to take action.

Given this one stark fact the police would immediately require further information. They would ask, 'What is the position now?', and this question encompasses other facts. Perhaps an ambulance has arrived. A police car may already be on its way. Traffic congestion is developing on the road where the accident occurred. Of course, if one took an aerial photograph of the scene a whole mass of detailed facts would be visible; the driver of one of the cars might be relieving himself behind the hedge, but this fact is irrelevant to the police in coping with the situation. This whole subject of the relevance of information, sieving the available data to select the information which is relevant, is a very vexed one which depends much more upon human discretion than on computerized condensation!

The facts outlined thus far gain greater significance when one relates them together to provide a picture of what is going to happen, or derive from one set of facts their implication for another situation.

To answer the question 'What is going to happen?' we need to explore other facts that, either through the passage of time or as a result of their functional relationship, are going to react on the situation caused by the car crash.

For example, the traffic density ten miles away provides information on how the traffic congestion problem at the scene of the accident is going to develop. Previous statistical analyses of the relationship between traffic congestion and accident rate will give some indication of the problem that is going to arise, and therefore the demands upon the traffic police, ambulance service and hospital facilities can be predicted.

By presenting individual facts—traffic density, accident rates, and so forth—in context, a context of time and functional interrelationships, one is able to provide those responsible for managing the situation— in this case the police—with information about what is going to happen in time for them to do something about it.

The final stage in this 'facts to information' loop allows them to explore the effects of alternative courses of action; it answers the question 'What would happen if . . .?' For example, a range of road blocks and diversion signs might be possible and it would be important quickly to select the most suitable.

The information used by the police in dealing with this all-too-frequent occurrence started out with the single data item which answered the question 'What has happened?'; the horizon of information about this event was extended as more complex questions were asked: 'What is the position now?' 'What is going to happen?', and 'What would happen if . . .?' All such questions are aspects of management information.

In pursuing the question 'What is management information?' we must explore the following facets.

First, let us consider a 'manager'. He is sandwiched between the information he needs concerning his job in order to control and manage it, and the requirements placed upon him by his superiors, or by the environment, to supply information about his job. Thus a manager is both a user and a supplier of information. Then we must examine the decision processes used by that manager: how he reaches his decision, and the information this process requires. Clearly no manager can be viewed in isolation. We have seen how he is sandwiched, and the way in which he is managed will have a considerable influence upon his information requirements. Information is only of value to a manager if he understands it. This understanding stems from two sources, his learning process and the way in which the information is actually presented; these points will be dealt with later in this chapter. This will be followed, in the next chapter, by a number of case studies illustrating information systems incorporating many of the facets already dealt with.

Only after this can the techniques for the provision of the management information be studied. From this the conclusion is drawn that these techniques incorporate the same sort of basic principles as those employed for the management of data. The identification of these basic principles will go a long way to direct the study and development of these techniques.

The management sandwich

I referred earlier to how a manager is placed in an information 'sandwich'. He is caught between the information he is required to provide because he is part of an organization, with his place in the management tree, and the information he himself needs concerning his function in order to control it.

Usually there is no clear distinction between these two categories of information, and because of the resulting compromise neither information requirement is adequately satisfied. However, these two needs are quite different and must be regarded as such when considering the provision of management information.

Whilst one is able to advocate flexibility in reporting, nonetheless clearly there must be some structure to the management reports, some hierarchy of information, which makes it possible to combine information about one function with information about another.

If one is to learn from history, history must be recorded in such a way that comparisons can be made. One is often tempted to react to a new situation by changing the basis of the reports, only to find that it is then no longer possible to form opinions based on the information in the new reports because no historical comparisons can be made. It may well become necessary to design new reports, but either these should contain the elements that existed in the old ones, or reports should continue to use the old format in addition to the new one. Clearly the former is a more satisfactory method.

The same logic must be maintained in the hierarchy of reports. It must be possible to justify the information available at one level by means of more detailed information available on a lower level; it would be nonsense for a sales director to receive a report showing that order taking was behind target unless there were supporting reports detailing the erring sales territories or products.

The reports presented at the top of the company must reflect a pattern of reporting throughout the various management levels in the company, so that a statement at the top can be justified lower down. Even if there was not a statutory requirement to keep records and present statements from them in a particular way, organizations would still have some formal structure of reporting. An essential ingredient is that they must incorporate a standard set of definitions. When one of these management reports refers to 'stocks' that word must have the same definition as when used by another management report from another area of the organization. An individual manager, when seeking information about his own functions, is at liberty to define the term 'stocks' in any way he chooses, but as soon as he uses it in a report that forms part of the management structure, he must conform to the standard definition.

A common danger with reports made available to the senior managers of an organization is that it may not be possible to support the information contained therein by more detailed information lower in the organization. One will often find a small body of experts compiling information for the board and for senior management. However, unless the same information is available to the line managers concerned, who are able to support it with more detailed information, much of the value of the information is lost. The line managers will be embarrassed by its existence and will challenge its accuracy; thus any attempt by the senior management to initiate action based on this information could well be thwarted by the line managers who will have to implement the action.

In general, the management structure of reports is restrictive rather than constructive. One can even argue that 'reports' or 'accounts' fall outside the scope of a book concerned with information, since they have the same kind of function as a man who knocks at the managing director's door and says, 'Good morning, Mr Managing Director. We've just gone broke. Did you know it?' However, since in so many situations they provide the only source of information, it is essential for me to discuss them here.

Accountants have developed a sophisticated discipline and set of rules which make them a reliable source of information on what has happened to an organization's money. Because of the pressure put upon them by the nature of their job, the accounting network of reports very often represents the most advanced information network available. Criticism arises when people try to stretch this network to serve more dynamic management information needs, and it is here that conflict arises with the head-on collision between the discipline of the accountant and the dynamics of the information needs.

A significant element of this clash was demonstrated earlier in the contrast between the record of a real event happening to a real thing (in the case of a finished product passing into stock) and the cost-accounting information derived from man hours spent and materials used, etc. to give a value to the products manufactured and in stock. It is this contrast between the reality and the accounting discipline that adds weight to the fat man who is sitting on the management sandwich! The manager in the middle wants to know what is really going on, and wants to tell his superiors what is really going on, but finds he spends too much of his time having to explain the difference between what *he* says the facts are and what the *accounts* show.

A key to this dilemma can be found in a corporate authority which establishes the structure and definitions of the terms to be used within the formal reporting network, and also a data base that provides the common source of information for these reports. Thus a financial (accounting) statement concerned with standard annual salaries, for example, can be and is matched with a statement of the number and movement of personnel. A corporate reporting authority is needed not only to establish the pattern of corporate reporting, but also to control the definition and codes of significant items that appear in the reports. In a large, multi-divisional, international organization there is a major problem in defining the relationship between the corporate body and the constituent units. A whole range of relationships exists, and the evidence which demonstrates the relationship in any particular case is the nature of reporting that the corporate body requires of the constituent units, and the extent to which the identifying and descriptive codes used are established and monitored at corporate level.

The existence of a central authority on codes, refining the definitions and allotting the codes, makes it possible to construct the management flow of reports from a stated selection of codes. The definition of the codes can and should be influenced by the needs of the reports, and so the two functions of reporting and code control need to live together.

If one accepts the principle of unique coding, then the existence of a data base allows the construction of the reports to be achieved by the automatic selection of the appropriate groups of codes, which thus extract the relevant elements of data, with the help of a conversion table.

So much for the top slice of the sandwich: the requirements for reports and information placed upon a manager by his manager and by a central reporting authority. Now let us turn to the bottom slice: the information a manager requires about the functions for which he is responsible. One should regard such a manager, be he managing director or clerical supervisor, as at the pinnacle of a function, requiring information about it unconstrained by any wider requirement.

Anyone experienced in the provision of information to satisfy such a need, is familiar with the stock reaction of a manager when faced with a new twist to a problem. This manager will come along and say, 'I want some more information. Please can I have a report looking like this?' The conscientious data-processing man, as a good servant of the company and determined to demonstrate the quality of his service, beavers away to produce such a return. In due course, with pride, he goes along to the manager and says, 'Here is the report you requested.' In most cases, where the sort of data-management utilities are not used (and this is 'most cases'), the report results from yet another patchwork unique programme slotted uneasily into the integrated scheme of things.

Events take several possible courses following the production of the report. The manager might say 'Thank you very much', go away and study it, and then telephone an hour later full of ire because it is not precisely what he wanted, or because it contains some erroneous information (despite the fact that his department was probably responsible for providing the data, he still blames the data-processing man for the erroneous information). More work and more attempts eventually result in a print-out that satisfies the manager; but by that time the problem has resolved itself and he now wants something quite different to help solve his next problem!

Alternatively, and all too often, a manager, knowing from past experience how lucky he is if he gets anything resembling what he thought he had specified, will gratefully receive whatever print-out appears, and pass it over to his clerical section, who will spend hours and days extracting and re-analysing the data to give it the form he really wanted.

Yet another reaction of a manager on receiving the print-out is that he no longer seems particularly interested, but points to a dusty corner and says, almost casually, 'Thank you. Put it over there. Now will you please produce it for me once a month.' Once a month the report is produced and despatched to this manager; the dusty pile in the corner grows; the manager moves to another job or leaves the company; but the routine for producing the report grinds on. It is only when a major revision of the system takes place, requiring a review of all the outputs, that the waste involved with this report becomes clear and action is then taken to stop it. It is a salutary experience to undertake an output audit of all regular reports or print-out: to follow each copy and look critically at what is done with it. If the organization is large, a surprising number of the addressees will have since left, and an equally surprising number of the job titles no longer exist! A purging of this sort frequently brings about a substantial reduction in the number of reports produced, and also in their circulation, especially if one asks the recipient to justify his requirement. However, such a study also highlights the dissatisfaction and frustration of those managers who really need the information to help them do their job, but find that they never seem to get precisely what they want. Thus in this sort of situation nobody is really satisfied.

The preceding paragraphs might seem to be a plea for 'on-line' terminal interrogation facilities, but are certainly not intended as such. These facilities are explained and discussed later in this chapter, therefore comments here are concerned only with the nature of the problem and the logic of the solution rather than with a particular technique or piece of equipment.

The main theme is the provision of information to a manager, and in particular the information he requires about the function for which he is responsible. It has been frequently demonstrated how his requirement for information is frustrated by the compromise of routine returns purporting to satisfy many but in fact satisfying none. Hopefully also it has been demonstrated how the glib answer, 'What you need is a terminal in your office', all too easily avoids the real issue, which is how to design a system that does really satisfy the manager's requirement for information.

A useful technique is the 'information request form' (Fig. 5.1). This is a form specifically designed for an individual functional manager, on which he has to specify precisely what he requires. Instead of receiving routine reports, he receives nothing unless he specifies it, and in specifying it he has to detail the data to be included as well as the output format. This form needs some structure; it is certainly not sufficient to present the manager with a blank piece of paper and to tell him to write down what it is he wants to know. The structure of a form that has been used most successfully contains the following elements:

83

1. A range of output frameworks from which he can select the one he wants.
2. A defined number of character spaces he can use to describe the output, and which will appear as the main heading of the print-out.
3. Details of the data and possible groupings giving totalling levels, degree of listing or summarization, and so forth.
4. The sorting permutations possible, for him to choose the sequence which he wishes the print-out to adopt.
5. The parameters defining the data to be extracted, including the value limits—for example, a debtor analysis with parameters selecting all debts from a particular group of customers which are over six months overdue and where the total by customer number exceeds £5,000.

DEBTORS' REPORT

THIS FORM MUST BE COMPLETED ACCORDING TO THE USER'S GUIDE TO SPECIFY
SELECTIONS REQUIRED FOR STS 8 or STS9

1. RUN REQUIRED

STS 8 [ ] 1   or   STS 9 [ ] 2   No. of copies [ ] 77

2. REPORT HEADER

3

[grid of character boxes]

3. DATA TO BE PRINTED

a (i) Individual items to be listed [ ] 4   b Company required (i) Parent [ ] 7

(ii) Account totals only [ ] 5   (ii) Ingestormatic Ltd. [ ] 8

(iii) Account alpha totals only [ ] 6   (iii) Ingestorset Ltd. [ ] 9

4. FILE SEQUENCE

10

	1	2	3	4	5	6
Account no.						
Date (ascending)						
Date (descending)						
Invoice type						
Sales area (UK)						
Sales area (Overseas)						
Company group						
SIC code						
Payment terms code						
Special circs. dr.						
Debtor code						
Special circs. cr.						

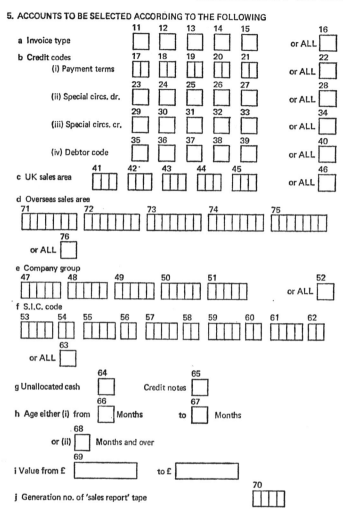

Fig. 5.1

Given such a facility the manager is made to think carefully through his problem in defining the output. Typical experience is that initially managers will make a number of mistakes, and the early outputs will not be what they expected. Quite soon, however, they become very skilled and are able to extract from the data base precisely what they require. Clearly there are more complex information needs which such

85

a system will not satisfy, or perhaps the manager may wish to include data that is not covered by his request form, and it is in these situations that he calls for assistance from an expert. However, the freedom he feels once he has gained experience in this technique is quite remarkable, as he is able to use the information available to him to help him do his job in a way that he can understand and control. He really feels in command of his data and can talk with confidence about 'his data base'.

A similar approach can be adopted through a computer terminal, however one needs to balance the need for 'instantaneous' information against the restrictions imposed by terminal use. Experience suggests that the freedom offered by filling up a request form and maybe waiting a day rather than having to accept the restrictions of the techniques of terminal input/output in order to obtain the information instantly, also the technical problems are less—a bird in the hand . . .

It is essential that a management information system should not remove from a manager the responsibility for his function, for providing information about it and interpreting this information. It is dangerous, in any but the simplest situations, to remove the interpretation aspect from the flow of information. Whilst there must be clear-cut statements of incontrovertible facts, it is rash to assume that any one man up the management tree can comprehend the implication of all these facts or be aware of the background to the particular situations they represent. To preserve some sanity in a management situation there needs to be a restriction upon the range of information available to each person and, where appropriate, information when supplied should indicate the originating authority and the name of the person who can provide the background and interpretation. The telephone and the memorandum are very necessary ingredients to a successful management information system.

When describing the management sandwich and the two sorts of information, a complex organization has been assumed. Most of the study that has taken place has been undertaken on simple single data-stream situations, which are the exception rather than the rule, and as they have only one basic stream of data, the problems of interpretation are not so great. Banks, airlines, railways, fuel-oil distribution are all examples of single data-stream organizations. Things are not so simple with local government authorities, companies manufacturing and marketing a diversity of products, armed services, governments. In these more complex organizations, anarchy in information is as dangerous as the anarchy of data arising from independent application-oriented data files. The manager must exist in a structure of information which has certain constraints and definitions imposed; but at the same time he must have great freedom in the way he can seek information from the activity for which he is directly responsible, always allowing for the interposition of interpretative information by managers at a lower level.

The use of terminals

A terminal is a small device that can link a person to a computer even if it is many miles away. It sends and receives messages to and from the computer and can make available to the user the range of facilities available in a computer and the data that is stored. Most airline offices now use such devices, usually looking rather like small television sets. The user can interrogate the data on the computer to find out, for example, if any seats are free on a particular flight, and they can send an instruction to the computer to reserve a seat.

Very often terminals are also found in scientific or educational establishments. Because they link the scientist to a computer, through them he can use the computer as a very powerful calculating machine. Usually these terminals are similar to typewriters: he types his problem and the answers are typed back so that he has a permanent copy of what he has done.

In both these examples, terminals provide the user with extremely valuable assistance. In the one case the booking clerk anywhere in the world has instant access to the latest reservation position on all the flights operated by that airline, and he can make instant reservations. In the other example the whole time-consuming chore of making long calculations is removed from the scientist.

There is no doubt that terminals will play an increasingly important part in the task of providing information and exploring the implications of that information. Already the use of visual display terminals to supply control information is commonplace in the management of such complex technological processes as space exploration, or on the control consoles of nuclear generating plants.

As a means of providing a wide-ranging and flexible information service, however, terminals have certain limitations. These limitations stem from restrictions inherent in such systems. The first arises from the way the data has to be structured on the file which is being accessed by the terminal. Here the situation is directly analogous to the restriction placed by a logical coding structure as compared with the flexibility provided by a unique coding system. To serve a terminal interrogation system and provide facilities to 'search' the data, this data must be

87

arranged according to a logical structure. This logic unfortunately presents a barrier to flexibility. Information which conforms to the logic can be provided, but as soon as the person using the facility is faced with anything out of the ordinary—a variation from his normal way of managing—the logic restricts him and the information system becomes a subject for abuse!

The second restriction presented by a terminal interrogation system arises from the means a manager has for communication with the system: he must do this through a keyboard. More advanced systems allow this communication to take place by using actual contact with items appearing on a visual screen, using either a light pen or touchwires; these systems have some potential but a lot of development and experimentation is still needed before this approach can be used as a flexible means of obtaining information from a data base. The normal access to the data is through a keyboard, and therefore the request for data have to be keyed in. In order to be keyed in they have to be coded in some way, and in order to code them the person using the facility needs to learn some interrogation language. Managers, in an information-seeking situation, resent the restriction of having to translate their information request into some form of interrogation language. They already have the problem of trying to sort out in their own minds what information they do require without the distraction of working out how they need to represent their request to the system. I have referred elsewhere to the development of problem-statement languages, and it may be that these will provide the means for a manager to express his information requirement in a form acceptable to the computer; there will then have to be a further stage in the development which will permit him to use such a language through a terminal. Thus this facility is two stages of development away.

The third restriction presented by terminal provision of information results from the output medium. There is a variety of output terminals, each providing a limited range of formats, but all have their restrictions.

The two most suitable for a manager's office (and of course the size and noise of the equipment are significant when considering this) are the ones I have already noted. By far the most attractive is the CRT terminal, or Visual Display Unit, where the information appears on a television-like screen.

These terminals, able to produce both tabular and graphical output, can be linked to some form of hard-copy output device, usually either photographic or typewriting. I hold a private view that these devices are going to proliferate in the years ahead, and will become as essential in a manager's office as his telephone. Not only will they provide him with ready access to his own filing system, but he will also be able to latch onto a whole range of information, subject only to appropriate human, logical and intellectual controls. A more usual type of terminal equipment is the conventional teletype or teleprinter one. Here the output is provided by a typewriter-like device that types out the information. Similar ones have been in use for a long time on the telex network and are familiar to most people. From the user's point of view they are far less attractive than a V.D.U., and all but the most modern are both noisy and slow, and their only attraction is their cost. In themselves they are cheaper than the visual units and they can make use of the cheaper telegraph circuits as compared with the telephone circuits needed by the others.

There are two other input/output devices which provide a user with access to a computer from his office. The first is the graphical display device which can present the output as a graph. This device plots a graph on graph paper in response to information transmitted from the computer. Graphically-presented information is a valuable way of displaying trends of information and therefore the device has its part to play in information systems. The alternative to plotting a graph on graph paper is to display it upon a special type of visual display screen (a storage tube terminal). In general this is more satisfactory, especially as hard copies can be readily reproduced photographically; but at present this equipment is rather expensive. Fig. 5.2 was produced by the hard-copy output device one can attach to such a terminal, and illustrates a style of graph that can be produced. It is in fact the graphical presentation of cash-flow information generated from a financial planning model developed by R. J. Haynes and A. H. S. Loh at Imperial College, with assistance from A. W. Foxworthy of ICL. The hardware used was a Tektronix D.V.S.T. Terminal and Hard Copy Unit connected to a P.D.P. 10 computer. One can expect that this type of visual display unit will become cheaper and thus more competitive with standard character-set device.

Finally, it is quite possible to use a normal computer printer remote from the computer itself; and, given suitable telephone lines, this can be put anywhere. It is of course large and noisy and therefore unlikely to be found in a manager's office; also it is usually associated with some input device such as a teletype terminal, or card or papertape reader. These in their turn would need to be provided with cards or paper tape which someone had punched, so they interpose many stages between the manager with his problem and the provision of the

89

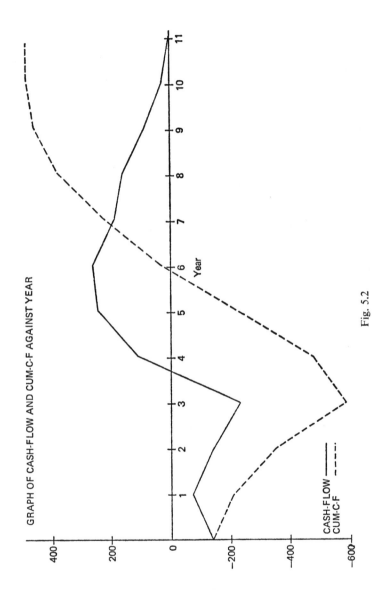

GRAPH OF CASH-FLOW AND CUM-C-F AGAINST YEAR

CASH-FLOW ————
CUM-C-F -------

Fig. 5.2

90

information through an output device in his office. However, this form of remote computing is becoming a pattern for the future, with large powerful computers linked to input/output devices in distant locations.

One of the case studies I describe in some detail in the next chapter is an information system which does use visual display units in directors' offices. Later in this chapter I will describe the Westinghouse scheduling system, but, in general, experience tends to support the view that there are as yet few effective management-information terminal systems. This does not mean to say that such systems will not come into being; but their obvious glamour should not distract us from answering the basic problem 'What is management information?' with a more comprehensive and realistic appraisal.

Information for the decision process

This book would be so easy to write if organizations were made up of entirely objective people who made completely rational decisions. However, this is not the case, and as a result the world is a fascinating place in which to live! Even if organizations *were* made up of entirely objective people, it would probably still not be possible to define the most rational decision about any particular set of situations. This is particularly so when decisions are taken which influence future events and which therefore must take into account the future interaction of circumstances. Sometimes, though rarely, these future circumstances can be precisely measured, as in the 'best-mix' sort of equation. Given known information on the characteristics of alternative constituent parts to a mixture that has to be produced, and a stated characteristic for the resultant mixture, then the most suitable mixture of components can be rationally established. However, even this simple situation is fraught with dangers; for example, one of the stated characteristics of the resultant mixture might be that it should be the 'most economical'. This introduces a nice exercise of judgement: a management decision requirement that has to establish what is meant by 'most economical'. Perhaps, although similar in effectiveness, the cheaper of resultant mixtures has worse preservation characteristics than the more expensive one, and so judgement has to be exercised on relative importance between cheap components and long-lasting mixtures. How long-lasting? What are the costs of storage? How far will the resultant mixture have to travel? How large is the present stock holding?

Into what started as an apparently simple rational process a number of variables have now been introduced, not all of which can be precisely stated and measured. And so the decision about which components to

91

usc in the end results from the opinion of the decision-taker, aided by such facts as are available; and any two 'objective' decision-takers will frequently hold different opinions!

Decisions range from those resulting predominantly or exclusively from precise measurable information, to those in which human judgement and opinion dominate; and the latter form by far the larger proportion of management decisions!

Organizations find it difficult to define their objectives. Commercial concerns have the spur of the measurement of 'profitability', but this can be expressed in so many different ways and is so influenced by the treatment of taxation or the evaluation of assets that it is rarely possible to use 'profitability' as a precise guide. Anyway, profitability when? A high profit this year and let next year go hang? A low profit this year so that a higher profit can be shown next year? A high capital investment programme for the next two years so that a substantial profit can be shown in five years' time? In non-commercial organizations it is even more difficult to define the objectives; what is the objective of the local government councils, or a government department, for example. I suppose one can define the objective of the armed services as 'to win the battle', but this is only valid when there is a battle to be won, and when one can define what is meant by 'winning'.

Professor Joad, in his Brains Trust days, established that in almost any human situation 'it all depends upon what you mean by . . .'.

So there we have it. Ill-defined objectives, non-quantifiable components, differing objective opinions—it is into this maelstrom that we wish to introduce management information! Information to aid effective decision-taking. Information to help a manager take better decisions. Not 'the best', not 'optimization', because both of these would require too precise a definition of the objectives. I am restricting this chapter to 'better' decisions, or perhaps only to permitting a manager to explore alternative decisions, so that he can use his judgement to select the most appropriate of the alternatives he has explored.

In a paper read to the I.F.I.P. Congress in Edinburgh in August 1968, Professor M. S. Scott Morton, of the Massachusetts Institute of Technology, outlined an interesting aspect of this choosing between alternatives. He was involved with J. A. Stephens of the Westinghouse Electric Corporation in developing a visual display system for the management planning function. A description of this system is contained in the papers of the Congress, but briefly it was concerned with the dialogue between the Marketing Manager and the Production Manager of the Laundry Equipment Division. The purpose of this dialogue was to determine the production and sales plans for the forthcoming months. The system enabled them to balance four complex sets of variables. They could compromise between:

(a) Expected demand
(b) Merchandising plans
(c) Available inventory
(d) Production availability.

These four sets of variables have to be balanced to provide some form of 'optimal' solution for Westinghouse. This solution consists of sales, production and inventory plans for each model of washing-machine, and its various colours. The aggregate of the models is, of course, the overall plan. Each of the variables is considered at each level of aggregation. What may seem 'right' at the model level may seem 'wrong' at the overall level. For example, the aggregate sales level may appear unreasonable, the total inventory too high, production levels too variable, or production capacity under- or over-utilized. This is a reasonably complex planning process.

I am including this example from Westinghouse because Professor Scott Morton's comments on the impact of this system on the decision process bear on my thesis that a manager needs information and techniques to enable him to explore alternatives. The following is an extract from Part III of the paper:

'The choice phase of the decision-making process was affected in that the managers would try several possible solutions for a particular problem. The manager remained the creative component of this system, but he appeared to be able to visualize the status of the problem more clearly with this system and could then suggest one, or several, other alternatives and try these out in turn. The system implemented his suggested solutions and allowed him to see the impact quite specifically. This led to a sharp reduction in discussion among the participants as to the likely impacts of certain alternative strategies, and the time in the decision-making process itself was spent much more productively.'

The Westinghouse experience has demonstrated that information systems cannot replace the decision-taker. They can support him but, as Scott-Morton says, 'The manager remained the creative component of this system. . . .'

Peter Cloot wrote in *Management Today*:

'The manager knows only too well that problems are only management problems if they cannot be clearly defined and relevant factors quantified. If they could be, they could be delegated to someone else, or even solved automatically.

'Much of the argument about whether computers should be allowed to "take decisions" would evaporate if it were recognized that it is really the criteria that are under discussion, not the decision itself. Of course, computers should be allowed to take decisions, in just the same way as clerks do; either can decide whether income tax should be charged at 6s or 8s 3d in the pound when calculating a payroll—provided the criterion of total taxable annual income exceeding £300 has been defined beforehand. But computer men are no more able to define decision criteria in management problems than the manager is entitled to abdicate their definition. In a manual system where a manager has delegated his responsibility too far, mishaps are often avoided because someone lower down the chain uses his judgement— but this safety feature is no longer available in a mechanized system.

'For decisions that do call for a manager's skill, all a computer system can do is present the information to him more effectively.'

The moral to be drawn from these two examples is that the taking of decisions is essentially a human activity, requiring discretion and judgement. The information system must support this process but can never supplant it. In the discussion on 'intercommunication', I isolated the dangers of delegating too much to 'the system'. The danger is not only that one has removed the possibility, as Peter Cloot says, of 'someone lower down the chain using his judgement', but also that the existence of precise numeric statements of alternatives deflect, in a subtle way, the decision-taker from considering his problem, to choosing between models!

The process of taking any decision frequently involves the decision-taker in the construction and use of a mathematical model. Of course he rarely identifies it as such and it is doubtful if he would recognize this description of his activity, but modelling it is. Take, for a simple example, a transportation manager. He may be required to move 50 tons of material. His mental model relates the capacity of his trucks to weight to be moved and he explores the alternatives of using one 10-ton truck for five journeys, five trucks for one journey, or some solution in between. Other relevant information comes into his calculation—return loads, availability of the trucks, and so forth—but the heart of his 'model' is the truck/load relationship.

Many millions of envelope backs are covered with calculations of this sort; some do not even require writing down, but all represent some form of mathematical modelling.

Understanding of these 'grass root' models and the operating relationship they identify is essential if the managers concerned are to receive information which is of use to them. If they receive it in a form that reflects their instinctive decision processes, they can understand it, and through understanding will be able to use it.

The next section deals with this subject more fully and shows how the information requirement is influenced by the modelling activity, and that these models need to reflect the way a manager thinks about his job.

How a manager is managed

You can take a horse to the water, but you can't make it drink—or can you?

When discussing the management sandwich it was necessary to consider a manager in two contexts: as an individual at the pinnacle of an activity, requiring information about that activity to help him manage it; or as a manager playing his part in a larger organization, interacting with other managers for whom he has no direct responsibility but with whom he must work effectively and where he must also conform to a corporate requirement and pattern.

It is important to separate the information requirements of a manager when he is solely concerned with his own management function, from the requirements influenced by his position within the organization. The way in which he himself is managed plays a very important part in influencing what he wants to know.

So many people talk about a management information system as if it was something that could be developed in isolation and independent of the circumstances in which it is going to be implemented. This is, of course, nonsense, and one cannot and should not separate the information system from the management control system. The information that flows must reflect and monitor the controls that are established, and these will vary from organization to organization and from year to year.

There is a whole body of theory concerned with how to manage an organization: Management by Objectives, P.P.B.S. (Planned Programmed Budgeting System), Fixed Budgets, Variable Budgets, Operational Plans, Corporate Plans. It is not the purpose of this chapter to debate the attributes of these theories; rather it is intended to demonstrate their influence on the information system.

95

To illustrate the point I will take as an example the simple case of a manager responsible for the inventory of spare parts required to service equipment sold and installed by his company. The management cycle starts (it is not strictly accurate to nominate any point in a cycle as the start but we must begin somewhere) with the exploration of the relationship existing within the total organization. Company planners, the economists, and the operational research men build models to reflect these relationships, and explore alternative courses of action. Amongst these models there will undoubtedly be one which explores the relationship between the population of installed equipment and the inventory of spares required to service it. The four variables with which we are concerned here are:

1. Growth rate and level of installed equipment.
2. Service level (down time, mean time between faults, or some such).
3. Relationship between inventory and population.
4. Operational cost relationship to total inventory.

Let us assume that item 2 is fixed, that the value for item 3 that we have chosen is a 5% relationship of inventory value to capital value of installed equipment, and that the operating cost for item 4 represents a 20% overhead on the inventory level.

If we set a growth rate of installed equipment which gives the capital value of installed equipment as £200 million at the end of planning year 1, then the planned spares inventory of 5% would be £10 million, and the inventory operating overhead (20% of inventory) would be £2 million.

This gives a basis for constructing the plan for year 1 for approval by the board incorporating these levels of activity: £200 million, £10 million, and £2 million.

Assuming the planners have done their job well, and that appropriate alternatives and key factors were submitted for board approval at the proper formative stages, then it is reasonable to assume that the board will accept this plan.

From the point of view of the management information system, the next stage in the cycle is crucial. The translation of the plan, backed by board approval and representing an expression of company policy and intent, into an executive instruction sets the whole pattern, not only for the information system but for the way the whole organization is controlled.

I will pursue two possible ways in which this can be undertaken in order to demonstrate my point. Control is normally exercised through the budget prepared by the accounts department. This would give the inventory manager a budget ceiling of £10 million with an operating expenditure of £2 million. The corporate reporting structure would measure the inventory and operating levels and comment on divergencies. This pattern is now set for the inventory manager, who establishes inventory and expenditure ceilings for his various depot managers; thus in the setting of the budget a structure has been created for the information system. Each manager monitors his inventory level and operating expenditure, and the accumulation of the reports from the various managers leads into the corporate information statements. If one assumes good management then one can expect the budget expenditure to be achieved: year-end inventories totalling £10 million with an operating expenditure of £2 million.

Most people would recognize this form of budgeting and budget reporting, but it provides a horrifying example of a complex web of budgets, targets, constraints and reports all built on one shaky assumption—the assumption that the population of installed equipment by the year end will in fact have achieved a capital value of £200 million. If this turns out not to be so, then the whole edifice comes crashing down. Harsh experience tells us that planned growth rates are rarely achieved, whereas expenditure ceilings are always achieved, if not exceeded. Thus I have just demonstrated a management system which could well result not in better control but in an increase of overheads by control of the wrong things.

The other approach is one which does not control the absolute levels of activity which result from the various calculations that take place whilst the plans were being formulated, but instead uses the factors that form the basis for these calculations. Thus an inventory of 5% by value of installed equipment becomes the budget, not an inventory of £10 million; operating expenditure at 20% of inventory levels, not £2 million. If these factors are expressed as part of the operating targets set, they have a marked impact upon the information requirement that is generated.

An inventory manager, and in turn the various depot managers who report to him, when given an operating plan which requires them to restrain the inventory to 5% by value of the installed equipment, will at once start asking questions about the value of installed equipment. Now instead of looking introvertedly at the value of spares in the various depots, they will be looking at the population these spares are meant to service. They will become outward-looking, and the whole organization comes alive by the simple expedient of presenting the operating plan as a

97

network of relationships that represents the relationship of one function to another.

The organization can now react intelligently to changing circumstances, as each manager is seeking information which allows him to control his unit as part of the whole organization, rather than as an isolated unit operating to sterile, absolute budget ceilings.

The management of the company also has gained in its ability to control the company; in a drive to increase efficiency, it can set an inventory target of 4·9 % of installed machines and monitor the progress towards achieving this.

A gulf exists between osteopaths, homoeopaths, surgeons, physiotherapists, physicians, psychologists, psychoanalysts, psychiatrists and the rest. If an osteopath were to propose a course of treatment for a patient it is probable that a practitioner in one of the other disciplines would not agree to pursue it.

This ogre of compartmentalization is ever-present and creates the barrier between the variable factors that go to make up a model and the absolute values that comprise a budget. It is a matter of different people trained in different disciplines: the old, tried and proven profession of accountancy entrenched in the citadels of conventional budgeting, and the upstart professions battling to construct operating plans which incorporate not only the absolute financial levels of activity but their relationships one to another.

It is my opinion that the solution to this conflict lies in how one organizes this control function within a company. The grouping together under one head of the activities of business planning, operating planning (incorporating the budget), management accounting, and the information service, makes a start for breaking down the compartmental barriers, but individual understanding and leadership still remain the key. The information a manager requires, particularly when he is regarded as part of the management structure in an organization, is greatly influenced by the way he himself is managed.

The learning process

The purpose of management information is to help a manager do his job regardless of whether he is a managing director or the most junior line executive. As indicated previously, his job consists of controlling the function for which he is directly responsible and also of conforming to a corporate pattern. Information to help him fulfil his function is only of value if it serves him, if he understands it and can use it.

98

This chapter is concerned with a manager's understanding of information and the use he can make of it, and a simple case study will illustrate the points I wish to make.

A data base had been successfully established serving a wide range of applications. Discussions were under way with the line managers about the sort of information they required from this base to help them manage the function for which they were responsible. One particular line manager insisted that he should receive, every month, a full print-out of that part of the data base for which he was responsible. This entailed a substantial detail listing, weighing several pounds, and of course in direct conflict with all the theories of good management.

However, that print-out was given to him, and for a number of months it arrived on his desk as a matter of routine. The reasons for giving him what he wanted were fourfold. The first was that it was essential to build up his confidence in the data base so that he could trust any subsequent extractions or analysis of the data therein. The second reason was that his confidence in the data-processing staff would be built up and he would see them as people who were there to help him do his job in the way he wished to do it; no purpose could be served by persuading or imposing upon him a pattern of management which he was not able or willing to accept.

The third reason was that the print-out did quite clearly reflect what he wanted to see; his was the responsibility for managing his function so it was his job to say what he required to help him manage it. The final and most important reason was that the full listing represented something that he could really understand.

This, however, was not the end of the matter. Rather it represented the beginning. Having retained his confidence by supplying him with the information he wanted, the data-processing staff were able to continue working with him on this print-out, helping him to use it. They were able to help him come to a better understanding of his job so that after a few months he asked, 'Wouldn't it be a good idea if you printed out only those items which are going wrong?'

His learning process had brought him to an understanding of an 'exception print-out', and through his experience of working with the detailed listing, the confidence he had developed in the data base and in the data-processing staff, he was now ready to work on an exception basis and could define the parameters within which the exceptions should be extracted.

The process of working with that manager, supplying him with what he wanted and helping him use it, was continued. As time passed he began to be able to identify the situations which caused the exceptions to occur some three months before they actually occurred, and he was able to specify an analysis which answered the question, 'What is going to happen?' This manager, who started by insisting upon a full listing as his only management report, now reached the stage of seeking quite advanced management control information.

The progress did not end there. To have a clear indication of what is going to happen leads on readily to the question 'What can I do about it?' The manager could now pose the 'What if . . .?' type of question and he constructed some simple models to help himself to explore various courses of action to avoid the exceptions actually arising.

It took over a year to help that manager progress from the detailed listing to posing the 'What if . . .?' questions, but, as a result, at the end of that year he was far better able to manage his function, using more sophisticated management control techniques than he could have done if he had been fully exposed to them right at the beginning.

The manager in question was quite unlearned in any management sense: he had left school at fourteen and had been working in industry ever since. Even now he does not hold a particularly senior position, but is a good, experienced manager who through the years has developed a very thorough understanding of his job. Despite all this it has proved possible for him to use advanced management information techniques, exception reports, predictions, and models.

This case study has been explored at some length because it illustrates a number of important aspects of management information and those concerned with providing it.

The first point that it illustrates is how the value of information to a manager depends absolutely upon the degree of his understanding of that information. It is quite useless, and even dangerous, to provide him with information he is not ready to receive. All too often his feeling of inferiority, when faced with those bright young computer men, will make him reluctant to betray his ignorance, and he will therefore signify his acceptance of proposed print-out format with no real understanding of its content. When the print-out comes along he may pay lip-service to it, but it is unlikely to contribute to his ability to manage, both because he does not fully understand it, and because its value suffers from the absence of his constructive participation in its formulation. The likelihood is that he will continue to manage in his old way and retain some duplicate records which he does understand and which he knows how to manipulate in order to get the information he requires.

The second aspect which the case study reveals is the contrast between the learning process of a line manager and that of someone trained in a more formal discipline. The scientist can progress in the understanding of a situation by reason and logic; from one set of facts he can deduce the next; he can explore mathematically the interrelationship of varying factors, and construct reasoned, logical, accurate solutions. The line manager on the other hand is beset with things to do. All the time he is reacting to circumstances; the interrelationships which are a set of equations to the scientists represent real life to the manager. He has no time to sit back and reason objectively about how he does his job, and even if he did he may well not have had the necessary training enabling him to subject his activity to objective scientific analysis. He performs his job using his experience, his knowledge of the job, his intuition, to arrive at reasonable, subjective, and often right, solutions.

The contrast between the accurate solutions of the scientist and the right solutions of the manager provides the greatest challenge of all to the management scientist, who has to combine the virtues of both to achieve for the manager the fastest possible understanding of the way in which he can use management information and use the techniques available to a management scientist, in order to improve his control over his job. Learning by doing, as in the case of a manager, may not be intellectually satisfying to the scientist, but woe betide the scientist who ignores the instinct and feel of a manager. It is these very attributes, transcending the exercise of logic, which lead to successful management. Having armed himself with the information available to him from a scientific analysis of the problem, a good manager then uses that most illogical of attributes—judgement. He allows all the facets of the situation, the illogical as well as the scientific, to help him reach a balanced judgement, and we are a long way from replacing his ability by scientific reasoning and electronic machines.

The third moral to be drawn from the case study is the varied nature of management information. It is apparent that for that manager the initial listing played as important a part in the 'management information system' as did his subsequent manipulation of alternatives through mathematical models. This reinforces the belief that there is no such thing as a management information system. To talk about it as a software package is absolute 'bunkrupt'! Management information requires that each stage in a manager's learning process be matched by information about his job that he can understand.

Presenting information

In presenting information, looks are extremely important. We frequently underrate the importance of appearance. The hysteria mani-

101

fested over long-haired youths (synonymous with pot, sex, orgy, vice, crime, filth, and so forth) demonstrates how appearance can affect our judgement. After all, Christ was long-haired and untidy; Hitler was short-haired and respectably dressed!

Some years ago I was responsible for proposing the manufacturing programme for a company and calculating the financial implications of this programme. The input to this activity was a sales forecast, combined with information on outstanding orders and stock holdings. On one particular occasion we received a sales forecast that had been prepared by the sales organization and was underwritten by the sales director. Details of this forecast are shown in Fig. 5.3 and you will see that I have provided comparative information on past achievement. My job was to recommend to the board the manufacturing programme that should be established to satisfy the forecast demand, and with a manufacturing lead time of twelve to fifteen months, once the board had given their approval substantial sums of money would be committed in raw material purchases and tooling up.

Our preparatory work showed us quite clearly that the sales forecast could not be right. It was wrong not only because it required a tremendous acceleration in the order-taking rate, but also because the forecast rate in the remainder of the current year would have to exceed the forecast rate for the following year.

Detailed examination of the figures in Fig. 5.3 makes this clear, but the manner in which these figures were presented does not. Our problem was that we had been given the forecast by the sales director and our job was not to criticize the forecast but present its implications in terms of manufacturing and gross profit. We felt, however, that it would be irresponsible of us to recommend a manufacturing programme to our board without making them question the validity of the sales forecast on which it was all based. The papers we compiled for the board included an expression of the sales forecast, Fig. 5.4, highlighting the contrast between actual achievement and forecast achievement. Within half an hour of receiving his copy of the board papers, the sales director withdrew his forecast and the item was postponed until the next board meeting.

There are two points to be drawn from this case study. The first is to re-emphasize the main theme of this section: it is the appearance that counts. The second concerns the danger of constructing sophisticated company plans, incorporating advanced mathematical techniques, and exploring a whole range of possible alternatives all based upon primitive and vague assumptions. I once worked for someone who delighted

102

ORDER LEVEL/FORECAST-by quantity
(including local manufacturing)

	1961–1962			1962–1963			1963–1964 Pds 1–4: Actual			1963–1964 Full Year F'cast			1964–1965		
	U.K.	EXP.	TOT.	U.K.	EXP.	TOT.	U.K.	EXP.	TOT.	U.K.	EXP.	TOT.	U.K.	EXP.	TOT.
Ingestors mk I 7-phase															
Model 302	214	121	335	172	99	271	42	20	62	120	70	190	100	50	150
Model 502	20	26	46	22	11	33	8	2	10	20	5	25	10	4	14
Model 502A	—	—	—	86	24	110	35	24	59	110	45	155	100	45	145
Ingestors mk I 10-phase															
Model 79	191	187	378	149	133	282	27	57	84	70	95	165	35	69	104
Model 90	—	—	—	30	6	36	27	9	36	70	14	84	70	14	84
Heavy-duty Ingestors															
Model 130	—	—	—	28	11	39	9	2	11	40	9	49	40	10	50
Model 131	23	18	41	—	2	2	2	2	4	17	14	31	15	11	26
Model 132	—	—	—	—	—	—	—	—	—	3	—	3	3	—	3
Model 150	17	12	29	30	28	58	4	9	13	25	23	48	15	18	33
Model 160	—	—	—	—	—	—	—	—	—	2	1	3	6	3	9
Model 190	—	—	—	—	—	—	—	—	—	14	2	16	18	-4	22
Model 012	—	—	—	—	—	—	—	—	—	1	1	2	2	—	2
C.E.G. Special	—	—	—	—	—	—	—	—	—	1	—	1	1	—	1

£'000s standard works costs

| Total value of all machines | 8,836 | 6,069 | 14,905 | 10,521 | 6,996 | 17,517 | | | | 15,176 | 7,578 | 22,754 | 14,885 | 7,001 | 21,886 |

Fig. 5.3 Left, past activity; right, forecast.

103

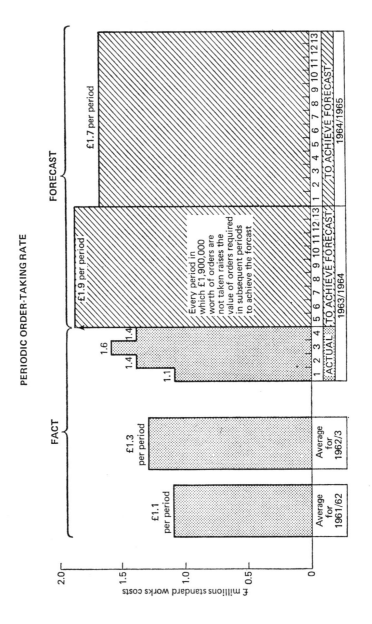

PERIODIC ORDER-TAKING RATE

FORECAST

FACT

£ millions standard works costs

Average for 1961/62
£1.1 per period

Average for 1962/3
£1.3 per period

1.1
1.4
1.6
1.4
1.4

ACTUAL

TO ACHIEVE FORECAST
1963/1964
£1.9 per period

Every period in which £1,900,000 worth of orders are not taken raises the value of orders required in subsequent periods to achieve the forcast

TO ACHIEVE FORECAST
1964/1965
£1.7 per period

Fig. 5.4

in the cleverness of his approach; he had constructed a system which took a whole range of subtle relationships and factors into account. He would happily work all night, encouraging his staff to do the same, producing reams of tables which set out the implication of a particular course of action, yet without devoting any thought or study to the validity of the basic assumption.

One could perhaps cite the National Plan produced soon after the Labour Party took office in 1964. Many years of calculation must have gone into its preparation, and it was a comprehensive document spanning the entire range of the nation's economy; but the whole thing fell into disrepute because the basic assumption of a 4% growth rate proved to be invalid!

Presenting information in a way that demonstrates the significance of the information, without either over-simplifying it or creating a misleading picture, requires special skills which not everyone possesses. It needs statistical understanding combined with a good eye for visual presentation. Any unit in a company whose job it is to analyse and present information should perhaps include on its staff the leaven of a commercial artist, or at least someone with an eye for presentation. The effectiveness of the unit will be vastly improved if the recipients of the information can immediately understand the message it contains.

Providing management information

The data base described in this book is more concerned with the logic of the data than with computers. Computers help, but understanding the nature of the data is paramount. Similarly one needs to understand the nature of information, and the variety of information situations demand more than a single logical structure.

The provision of management information requires the extraction, manipulation and interpretation of data. It is important that an information system is not burdened with too precise a conception of the information required as this will lead to inflexible file structures and inefficient interrogation techniques. A stipulation that the user must place upon the system is this 'expectation of change': a recognition that the best information frequently stimulates the recipient to ask for more and different information.

Given this initiative from the user and a sound data base there are a number of data processing techniques the D.P. professional can use in order to build this flexibility into the system. Some of these will emerge in the case studies which follow in the next chapter.

Chapter 6

Two Case Studies

A sales reporting and control system

It will be clear that there is no such thing as one comprehensive static management information system for a company. Nor is there a software package that can conjure up management information out of nothingness.

The ability to provide management information depends upon two facilities: the first is a source of reliable data and the second is the ability to present this data in a whole variety of ways to meet a whole variety of management information requirements. It has been shown that one needs to regard each manager in two contrasting situations: firstly, as a manager at the top of a function, requiring information to help him control that function; and, secondly, as a manager of a function which forms part of a larger activity and which needs to interact with other functions and other managers. The way a manager is managed will influence his information requirements, and an understanding of his decision process and the progressive developments of his learning process all influence the information he needs.

With all this as a general background a case study of an operating information system is now presented in some detail.

As already shown, the effectiveness of information increases as it moves away from the 'What has happened?' to the 'What is going to happen?' type of answer. Examine the reports prepared in any company on, say, its order-taking achievement, and one will observe many examples of the 'What has happened?', but few which explore the implications for the future. Fig. 6.1 represents a typical sales achievement report.

Even the starting point, 'An order has been received', can be re-expressed: 'At some future point of time committed output or stocks will be used to satisfy that order and money will be received.' Thus from the one present fact it is possible to explore several future facts, in this

106

example to examine the implications that order has on the output programme, and on future cash flows. Fig. 6.2 reflects this and shows the extent to which future planned revenue is covered by orders already taken.

At least Fig. 6.2 represents a more positive control statement in that it highlights what needs to be done in order to achieve the plan for the future, as compared with Fig. 6.1 which merely reports what has happened. However, the real question is not 'How many orders do we still need to take in order to safeguard our future revenue?' but 'What is the likelihood of taking those orders?'

When we looked earlier at the sequence which followed a car crash, the information then shown was very much concerned with two basic relationships: a relationship in time and a functional interrelationship. It is now intended to examine a whole sequence of events relating to order-taking and show how their relationships can be used to produce really effective sales-control reporting.

The sequence of events related to order-taking is made up from a number of activities, some of which take place before and some after the order itself is taken. First of all there is the identification of a prospect; this isolates the possibility of a future order. A prospect may be an existing customer who has old equipment to replace, or who wishes to extend or enhance his current range. He may be an organization with no equipment at all, or he may have a competitor's equipment installed.

Once identified, there are the events which lead up to the making of a quotation. The sales staff must identify and establish contact with the 'decision-taker', they must study the customer's problems, prepare with his staff a feasibility report, and finally submit a formal quotation or respond to a call for tenders. The quotation may or may not be successful; it may result in an order being taken or the order may go to a competitor. On the other hand the results may be indecisive and the whole matter deferred.

If the order is taken, production resources need to be allocated to satisfy that order; output schedules may have been committed in advance of actual order-taking and the correct mix of equipment has to be allocated to that particular order for delivery within the agreed time scale. The negotiation must be completed so that formal contracts are agreed, perhaps incorporating progress payments. In good time before the due date, the equipment is moved to the packing bay, packed, despatched, and subsequently it arrives on the customer's premises. Once there it has to be installed and the customer satisfied that it is working properly.

107

The invoicing procedures have to be followed, the correct charges raised; perhaps progress payments are involved, with subsequent charges upon installation and continuous charges for rental or leasing, and maintenance.

The sales activity could be said to span the sequence of events, starting with the identification of a prospect and ending with the invoicing that follows installation. (Of course, once equipment is installed with a customer, he immediately becomes a prospect for enhancement or replacement business, so the whole cycle repeats itself.)

Control of the sales activity starts with a company requirement of a gross revenue target. The sales organization must provide substance to that target by specifying the equipment that needs to be installed and revenue earning in order to achieve that target. The sales-planning activity works backwards from this and uses a sales simulation model which identifies the following events and factors:

EVENTS

Equipment invoiced
Equipment installed
Equipment despatched from works
Contract signed
Order taken
Quotation accepted/rejected/decision deferred
Quotation submitted
Survey undertaken
Prospect identified

FACTORS

Cash receipt delay (for liquidity control)
Invoice delay
Installation delay
Despatch delay
Average customer delivery delay requirement
Quotation success rate
Quotation to order delay
Surveys resulting in quotations.

The system uses four of these events: prospect identification, submission of quotation, taking of order, and installation of machine. It uses the various factors listed to calculate the consequential situation following any one of these events. The sales management establishes the matrix of events and factors that will satisfy the company's gross revenue target in a way they feel can be achieved, and then month-by-month sales activity is recorded against these events and the various factors. This information forms the input to the sales simulation model which is then used to forecast the order and delivery pattern over the forthcoming months. For products with fairly lengthy delivery cycles, this forecast can give a very good picture of orders and deliveries (hence revenue) up to twelve months ahead.

Fig. 6.1   Achievement: year to date orders taken

Product	Orders taken	Budget	Variance
Ingestors 10 ph	75	60	+15
Ingestors 20 ph	123	152	−29
Ingestors 30 ph	16	16	−1
	(etc.)		

Fig. 6.2   Achievement: orders against planned revenue

Product	Planned revenue earning despatches for next 12 months	Orders held against planned despatches	Orders still to take to secure revenue
Ingestors 10 ph	100	30	70
Ingestors 20 ph	200	120	80
Ingestors 30 ph	35	15	
	(etc.)		

Fig. 6.3   Sales management control return: position in twelve months' time

Products requiring management action	Forecast shortfall of revenue despatches	Reason	Plan	Actual
Ingestors 10 ph	15	1. Success rate	75%	60%
		2. Delivery required	6 months	10 months
	(etc.)			

Using this system it is possible to produce a sales control report which isolates those major items in the product range where the gross revenue target twelve months ahead is not likely to be achieved, and explains why. An example of such a report is shown in Fig. 6.3 above. If you compare it with the earlier example shown in Fig. 6.1 you will see that the fundamental difference is that, whereas Fig. 6.1 records what has happened, after the event, when nothing can be done about it, Fig. 6.3 isolates those situations that will result in something going wrong

109

twelve months hence, and does so in such a way that the reason is apparent. Thus the management have time to do something about it, either by influencing the selling activity, or revising the revenue forecasts so that expenditure ceilings can be adjusted before all the money is spent.

Theory, however, has to be exposed to the harsh light of practice, and real life is full of surprises and imprecisions. Two isolated situations will demonstrate this. First there was the occasion when the system demonstrated quite clearly that the target revenue would not be achieved for a particular product group. The sales management reacted, mounted a selective sales campaign, and retrieved the situation. Unfortunately, putting the spotlight on one particular product group took it off all the others, and business in these other areas suffered accordingly! The other occasion was when the system demonstrated that there would be an appreciable shortfall of revenue. The sales management confirmed this and felt they could do nothing to retrieve the situation. Expenditure ceilings were therefore reduced for the sales activity. It subsequently transpired that business perked up, the gross revenue was achieved, but on a lower sales overhead. The managing director was delighted but the sales director was most embarrassed!

This case study has described a sales control system which is used. It provides sales management with very useful information which they employ to control the sales function, and it contributes to the company's ability to manage its total operation by providing information about what is going to happen in time to react to adverse trends.

The Management Terminal System: introduction

There is much discussion on the value of supplying senior management with access to information through a visual display unit. Some of the issues were debated in an earlier chapter; however, no one can deny that management has an information requirement and a communication problem.

This chapter describes a case study with the minimum of comment; I hope through this description, and through continuing experience of operating this system, much will be learnt about the problem, and about the contribution which the facility to ask questions and have the answer displayed on a T.V. screen can make to the major problem of how to manage large companies.

This particular system operates for the company directors. Each director has in his office a visual display unit (V.D.U.), which gives him access to a wide range of information. Before actually describing the

110

system in detail, a fundamental principle that has been adopted needs to be emphasized, which overrides the freedom of interrogation and response. This is that the system must support the delegated authority of management: it must not allow the directors to short-circuit the management structure and undermine the authority of the individual line managers. The principle operates in two ways: there is a restriction placed on the questions each user can ask, and there is a restriction on the information that will be available.

To illustrate the first restriction, the following is a possible sequence of interrogations. The Managing Director interrogates the system for the value of orders taken. The summarized information which is displayed raises a query in his mind, and so he searches the system for more information on the subject. Although technically the system offers a considerable range of searching possibilities, his search will be halted at some stage by an answer appearing on the screen which tells him that if he wants any more information he must ring up the Marketing Director. This telephone call takes place, and the Managing Director tells the Marketing Director to look at the answer to a particular question. He does this and gets on his screen precisely the same image as is appearing on the Managing Director's screen. (This simple situation is of surprising value: a conversation between two directors over the telephone, about a set of figures, taking place without any danger that they might be looking at different figures. One recalls Lord Mountbatten, in one of his television documentaries, taking us round the Combined Operations Control Room and pointing to a film screen at one end. He explained that they could project a map on this screen and discuss their plans with absolute confidence that their commander in a remote location would be using an identical map.)

Like the Managing Director the Marketing Director has information available to him, but some is different from that available to the Managing Director as he has a different job. He searches his information and finds the answer to the question raised. Having found the answer he can then make that answer available to the Managing Director by permitting him to ask that particular, more detailed question. They can then discuss this answer, with the Marketing Director providing any interpretation that is necessary. Thus, although the information in response to the Managing Director's original problem is in the system, the Managing Director does not have access to it unless the director responsible for the particular function 'opens' the answer to him. One could say that this is an example of conversational computing, with the conversation between intelligent human beings providing interpretation

111

for the information. This system, therefore, is operating a two-way restriction on access to information, both upwards and downwards.

The second fundamental restriction is on the way in which information gets into the system in the first place. There is always a serious danger, in any system that supplies information to senior management, that the individual line executive can undermine their confidence in the system by casting doubts on the accuracy of the information. One of the things this system strives to avoid is the danger of such wrangles once the information is used outside the confines of the company directors. All information provided through the system clearly indicates the source, and information about operational activity will not be provided unless the line executive concerned accepts the responsibility for supplying the information or underwrites the accuracy of the source. When, therefore, executive instructions come down the line, or further queries are raised, instead of saying, 'The information is all bunkum', the line executive says, 'Yes, I know, because I understand and accept responsibility for the way in which the information was compiled.' One could argue that the line executive is therefore in a position to ensure that certain information never reaches the top level, but in practice this is not the case, as once the requirement for the information is raised with him, it is a brave executive who is prepared to deny the directors information for which they have stated a requirement. Another danger is that the executive might provide misleading information; however, as the source of the information is the data base, and there is an independent team working with him preparing the parameters for extracting the data, this is not likely to happen.

The physical structure of the system is now explained, showing how it works and outlining the range of logic-searching facilities available.

The system is built around an 'answer file' which contains the answers to predetermined questions. At no time does the system construct an answer in response to interrogation; it retrieves the answer, and clearly can only do so if the question has been anticipated. The interrogation language leads the user to the range of questions available on the topic of his choice, and then asks him to nominate the question he wishes to ask by inputting the question number. The answers are stored as 'frames' or visual images, and by inputting the question number the user accesses that particular frame, which is then displayed on the screen.

However, this first display represents the tip of quite a large iceberg! There are four dimensions in which the user can now progress, and the first three are as follows:

SINGLE GENERATION WITH 3 FRAMES

FRAME 1 CONSOLIDATED PROFIT AND LOSS ACCOUNT

FRAME 2 CONSOLIDATED BALANCE SHEET

FRAME 3 HOLDING COMPANY BALANCE SHEET

FOR A FURTHER BREAKDOWN OF THIS QUESTION
SEE QUESTION 300

ICH ANNUAL REPORT AND ACCOUNTS   ⌐

Z97/01/1   CONSOLIDATED   ANNUAL REPORT

	PROFIT AND LOSS ACCOUNT	£000	
		1969	1968
TURNOVER		115,361	92,181
LESS PRVN.-DEPRC'ION	15,175		11,697
COST-SALES/RSCH	92,749	107,924	74,721	86,418
		7,437	5,763
COMP.LSNGS.DIVDS.		1,710	1,172
TRADING SURPLUS		9,147	6,935
INTEREST PAYABLE		3,380	3,014
PROFIT BEFORE TAX		5,767	3,921
TAXATION			
PROFIT FOR THE YR		3,357	2,725
APP.TO RESERVES		1,264	104
DIV'DS BEFORE TAX		2,010	1,805
UNAPPROPRIATED			
PROFIT FROM PREV YR		1,727	911
BALANCE IN			
BALANCE SHEET		1,810	1,727
ICH ANNUAL A/CS	DOWN FOR BALANCE SHEET		⌐

VII   Showing (*above*) the definition frame for question 297 and (*below*) the first level of detail for this question.

```
300▮          SUMMARY OF ASSETS


        SINGLE GENERATION WITH 3 FRAMES

    FRAME 1 CURRENT ASSETS
          2 DEFERRED ASSETS
          3 FIXED ASSETS


        TOTALS C/F TO BALANCE SHEETS
        IN QUESTION 297

        FOR LIST OF MAIN DEBTORS
        CONTACT CHIEF ACCOUNTANT

        01-7188 7436 EXT 414


    BOARD RETURN 29                                    ⌐


300/01/1          SUMMARY OF ASSETS
            CURRENT ASSETS & LIABILITIES  £000
    .  .                               CONS'D VARIANCE
ASSETS STOCK & W.I.P LESS PROVS
       AND PROGRESS PAYM'TS             50,575    --
       DEBTORS & PREPAYMENTS            40,674    381
       BANK AND CASH BALANCES             812      8

       TOTAL CURRENT ASSETS            92,061    389

LIAB'S CREDITORS & ACC'D EXPS.         18,317    458
       BE CO. LTD. PAYABLE 8/70         1,500  1,500
       DEVELOPMENT FUND                 3,864    --
       TAXATION                           491    --
       PROVISIONS                       2,385    --
       FINAL DIVIDEND                    1,265  1,265

       TOTAL CURRENT LIABILITIES       27,822  3,223

  TOTAL C/F TO BALANCE SHEETS Q 297    64,239 (2,834)  ⌐
```

VIII Showing (*above*) the definition frame for question 300 and (*below*) the first level of detail for this question.

1. The information displayed could well represent a substantial con-
   solidation, and by typing the input message 'down' he can call up
   more detailed information. For example, the first frame might
   contain 'Total Orders'; going down might call up 'U.K. Orders',
   and down again 'Export Orders'. This same facility of 'down' can
   also be used for listing if there is too much information to be
   contained in one screen.
2. Rarely does information have meaning in isolation; more usually it
   needs to be presented in a context, often a context of time. The
   action of asking a question calls up the 'current generation' of the
   answer and on each updating the current generation moves back
   one, thus creating a 'past generation'. By inputting 'back' the user
   can access these past generations, and he can go back as far as the
   information is stored.
3. The company operating the system insists that any management
   report must contain not only 'actual to date' information compared
   to budget, but also forecast information, and to match this the
   system allows the user to input 'on'.

The system does not impose any restrictions on the number of frames
or generations and is so constructed as to make it very easy for the user
to move between frames and generations. In addition to 'down', 'back'
and 'on', he has other action verbs.

'*top*' will bring him from wherever he is to the first frame of the
generation he is interrogating.

'*now*' will bring him from wherever he is to the top frame of the current
generation.

'*prev.*' will display on the screen whatever image was there last and
is a very useful facility for see-sawing between questions if the user
wishes to compare two answers.

It is also possible for a user to nominate any individual frame in the
matrix and leapfrog straight there.

I said there were four dimensions and have listed three. The fourth
dimension is perhaps the most interesting; it certainly contains the
greatest potential for logic and reasoning. One of the difficulties to be
overcome in any information system is to ensure that the user has a
clear understanding of the question being asked. Both the index of
questions and the headings in the answers frame may well need amplification, and to obtain this amplification the user requests the particular
question but inputs a '?' after the question number. Instead of accessing
the answer, this instruction calls up a definition frame, and it is the way

in which one can use this definition frame that opens up a range of interesting possibilities. Three of these are listed below.

1. Definition of the terms and values used.
2. Clearly specifying the source of the information, and the source of more information outside the system.
3. The logic of the question showing how the question is constructed and the identification of the component questions. This definition frame can thus be used to indicate the hierarchy of information and opens the door to a whole range of more detailed questions and of course to their definition frames detailing their hierarchy, and so on.

The aim in designing this system has been to provide one which was easy to use and at the same time contained facilities in advance of the user's requirements. This allows those whose job it is to manage a company and solve its business problems to concentrate on those problems, rather than restrict their thinking by technical computer distractions.

What questions do they ask? In most companies there is a small body of people who spend most of their time preparing information for the board. I am not referring to the secretarial activity but the backroom statistician and financial analysts. The original range of questions was compiled in close collaboration with these people, drawing from their experience of the sort of questions the board members seem to ask. One can really divide the questions into groups. First there are those questions which regard the system in much the same way as a secretary uses her filing system. Routine returns can be displayed and access provided to previous issues of these returns; increasingly conventionally-presented returns, typed or reproduced on paper, are being replaced by the system which provides the directors' only means of access to these returns. There is quite a volume of these and it is now a very simple matter for a director to call up a particular return for a particular period or month, much as he would ask his secretary to extract one from her file. Once on the screen he can hop backwards and forwards, comparing that month with previous or subsequent months, or search out related information.

The second category relates to statements of rapidly changing situations: bank balance, updated each morning; own and competitors' share prices updated several times a day. Once again, with both of these it is useful to be able to move about in time to explore the trend. Of course, a flippant use of this type of information is to display such items of daily news as the cricket scores. This flippancy suggests the third category of information, which regards the system as providing a convenient means of communicating interesting information. Good examples here are newspaper abstracts from the daily press, and relevant references to government debate or recent legislation. Each user has the opportunity of providing information for a 'News of the Day' screen. This gives him the opportunity of ensuring that his colleagues know of significant events with which he is concerned: it may be the marketing director announcing he has won a large order, or that he is going to be visited by a particularly important customer or government official. It could be the manufacturing director announcing that the first-off of a new product has just successfully completed its quality control checks and that the green light has been given to quantity production. The experience of Control Data Corporation, in using similar terminals in top-level offices, suggests this is a popular facility with the directors, as currently they have no other way of ensuring that this sort of information is readily available to their colleagues.

The illustrations on Plates VII and VIII present aspects of the system used by the directors of International Computers Limited. Much of such information is, of course, highly confidential and so the choice has been limited to that which is publicly available.

An important feature of any such system is the strength of its security protection, and the user's confidence in this is essential if the system is to be fully exploited. The system would usually operate at three types of location, and it is necessary to consider the security aspects at each type. First, there is the computer itself, to which all the terminals are connected. Second, there needs to be some form of control centre; this includes the master V.D.U. which is used to control the total operation and is often the only one that can be used to input data; all the others, after the identification routines, can only input interrogations. The third type of location is represented by the user terminals themselves. These could well be some distance both from the other two locations, and from each other. The link between these locations is over the Post Office telephone lines, perhaps using a private network, or such a system can also work through the normal public subscriber-trunk-dialling complex.

User security is entirely under the control of the user. He has an identifying code which he must use to gain access to the system through any of the terminals, and which provides the key to the particular questions he is allowed to interrogate. This key operates very much like the combination number of a safe; at any time any user can change his code and is encouraged to do so after every session, or if other people have been present whilst he has been using the terminal. A person can

115

only break into the system if they know a user code, and they have to know it precisely because the system will automatically lock a particular terminal on the fifth unsuccessful attempt at identification. Once locked out, a user must contact another user who can arrange to unlock the system for him—once satisfied that the person locked out is an authorized user!

Security at V.D.U. control is more of a problem as it is less easy to control automatically through the system. The control centre is in a locked office, and access is restricted to nominated people. Within the office there are special arrangements for security waste, and there is a roster of authorized people who must be in attendance whenever the system is in operation. The connection of all the V.D.U.s to a power supply is through lockable special-purpose plugs and sockets, so once a terminal is switched off, it is also locked off, and only the person with the key can reconnect it to the electricity supply.

There are three ways of providing input to the system. Information can be called from the data base already on the computer, and formulated through a translator programme into the format of an answers frame. This sort of input does not present a major security problem as it is an automatic process. Other information can be input direct by V.D.U. control, and the security routines operating in V.D.U. control cover this activity. However, quite a volume of input is done as a batch-processing operation overnight, using eighty-column cards punched from information provided by various sources. To control the security of these, special input procedures have been adopted so that in fact all those handling the cards would be unable to establish their meaning. The input is dealt with in two stages: all the headings and descriptive matter is input to the system through the V.D.U. control terminal, and the cards that are punched contain only a jumble of figures which have no meaning until associated, within the computer, with the descriptive information.

One final link in the security chain concerns the communication of information outside the computer, in particular 'off-line' print-outs sent from the computer to V.D.U. control. Security at the computer is exercised through locked cabinets which contain the magnetic recording media when the system is not in use, and locked bags for the transmission of material to and from the computer. Only nominated staff have access to the keys to these cabinets and bags, and nominated senior staff have to be present when the system is in operation. It may seem that these security arrangements are excessive, but it is absolutely essential that the users have complete confidence in these security arrangements if proper use is to be made of the system. To ensure the continued maintenance of these security arrangements, the company security officer undertakes periodic security audits.

The Management Terminal System: operation

The Management Terminal System is operated on ICL visual display units coupled with hard-copy print units. The illustrations on the following pages go through a typical series of interrogations, shown as steps with explanatory notes, and are reproduced from the relevant hard-copy printed output.

The system in its normal use contains much highly confidential information; the examples here given come from a series of carefully edited demonstration questions. Each 'screenful' of information is referred to in this text as a 'frame', and this term is used frequently on the following pages. An ICL visual display unit is illustrated in photograph II opposite page 16.

The Management Terminal System described in the preceding chapter is an operational system. It first went on-line in June 1970 and, at the time of writing, use of the system continues to increase as well as the number of users connected to it. At its inception one would expect a degree of enthusiastic activity as the users played with their new 'toy'. The extent to which use has increased rather than decreased long after its inception indicates to what extent the users no longer regard it as a toy, but are beginning to consider a visual display unit beside their desk as much a part of their daily business life as the telephone or the dictating machine.

There are many critics who suspect that such a system represents pure gimmickry. There are even those who confuse a device which helps a manager obtain the information he wants with a 'magic machine' generating 'instant decisions'. This critical reaction is not unlike the reception given to the early motor-cars. Nowadays we do not question a man's desire for a motor-car; we do not call upon him to justify his need to travel from A to B before he buys one. We accept the motor-car: it is part of our daily life and we enter into no elaborate exercise to cost-justify the advantages of the motor-car over the horse, or over travelling by foot. In the same way, the time is not far off when we will accept the visual display unit as a device for presenting us with information. The V.D.U. makes no more contribution to solving the problem of *what* information we need than the motor-car makes to solving the problem of where to go—they are both devices which help us to achieve objectives *we* set.

117

Step 1

When a user's terminal is idle, either at the start of the day before he has entered the system, or when he has entered 'OFF' at the end of a session, the screen displays the instruction 'SIGN IN, PLEASE'.

INTERNATIONAL COMPUTERS LIMITED

I.M.I.S.

MANAGEMENT TERMINAL SYSTEM

SIGN IN, PLEASE

The system is designed on a very personal basis: each user has his own identifying procedure and his own set of questions.

There are three types of identifying codes. In general, the only code a user needs to remember is his own particular one; this operates like the combination number of a safe, and he is encouraged to change the combination frequently. In addition, each user has a unique user number. This number never changes; it is used for certain purposes within the system, and is needed for certain routines outside it.

The third code relates to the visual display unit: each of these has its own code number. To enter the system the user types in his own identification code, and this will cause the next image to appear.

Step 2

The user has now gained access to the system. As the system is personal to each user, in addition to his identifying code the user must

```
                INTERNATIONAL COMPUTERS LIMITED

                            I.M.I.S.

                 MANAGEMENT TERMINAL SYSTEM




         READY FOR INTERROGATION
```

remember the question number of his personal index. Although there are considerable searching facilities, all answers have been pre-formed and appear as the response to a particular question number. Apart from the number of his personal index, which the user must remember, the system leads the user to the question number which will retrieve the information he requires. Of course, through frequent usage a user will get to know certain key question numbers, and will be able to key in their numbers directly without going through any searching procedure.

Step 3

There are two levels of index.

On inputting the index numbers of his personal index, the user gains access to a list of chapter headings. Against each chapter appears the location of the frame containing the index of detailed subject headings within that chapter. By inputting the action letter shown he gains access to the detailed index he requires.

For example, by inputting the letter B for B(ack) he gains access to the detailed subject index for EXTERNAL DATA.

MARKETING DIRECTOR'S SUBJECTS

SUBJECT	INDEX LOCATION
INTERNAL DATA	O(N)
MARKETING	
FINANCIAL	
EXTERNAL DATA	B(ACK)
GOVERNMENT	
COMPETITIVE ECONOMIC	
GENERAL	
THE MANAGEMENT TERMINAL SYSTEM	D(OWN)
OPERATIONAL ADVICE	

Explanatory note 1

In addition to locating a particular frame by its question number a user can move from one frame to another by inputting the first letter of the appropriate action instruction, such as O(n), B(ack), and D(own).

By inputting his index number, the user has gained access to four or more frames of information. If they were all displayed at the same time, their arrangement would be as shown below.

Examples of the contents of the index frames are given on the following pages.

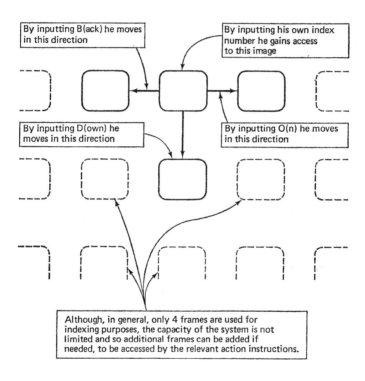

121

Step 4

Each chapter contains a list of subjects and each subject is identified by a question number. These lists are quite flexible; new chapters and new subjects within chapters can be, and are, added very readily. Likewise existing headings can be deleted.

The activity of the system is automatically monitored, and records are maintained of the number of times each frame is accessed. Clearly if one is only rarely accessed it becomes eligible for deletion. On the other hand, if it is accessed frequently this could indicate more information of related subjects would be of value.

Apart from this routine, monitoring contact is maintained with the users. This gives them an opportunity to react to the information available to them, and the system is designed to be sensitive and to respond to their reactions.

EXTERNAL DATA
YOU HAVE THE FOLLOWING OPTIONS:

GOVERNMENT
    22   GOVERNMENT MINISTERS
    45   DEPARTMENT OF TRADE AND INDUSTRY
    57   CIVIL SERVICE DEPARTMENT
COMPETITIVE/ECONOMIC DATA
    30   ECONOMIC DATA BY COUNTRY
    33   SHARE PRICES
    34   U.K. ELECTRONIC INDUSTRY PUBLISHED A/CS
    35   USA ELECTRONIC INDUSTRY PUBLISHED A/CS
    39   ELECTRONIC INDUSTRY MARKET
    47   USA BASED OPERATIONS
    49   COMPETITIVE INFORMATION
    54   CURRENCY CONVERSION RATES
GENERAL
    66   BIRTHDAY HONOURS LIST
    99   DIARY OF FUTURE EVENTS

O(N)=INDEX LOCATION

Explanatory note 2

By inputting the relevant question number, the user gains access to that subject. Two subjects are illustrated on the following pages: question number 45, Department of Trade and Industry; and question number 33, Share Prices. These are preceded, however, by an explanation of how, by inputting a question number, a user gains access to a subject rather than just one question. In fact, having 'located' a subject by inputting a question number, the user can search through that subject in four dimensions.

By inputting a question number, the user accesses a matrix of frames. The illustration below sets them out as if they were all displayed at once, and indicates that there is no technical restriction of the number of frames within a matrix. Each question number is supported by a matrix whose size is dictated by the needs of the particular subject; if those needs change, so the size of the matrix can be changed.

At its simplest one can view each matrix as a lot of unique pigeon holes. The user can travel between these pigeon holes freely by using certain action instructions, and he can move from one matrix to another by inputting a new question number. Into this very flexible framework the information scientist and the user are free to decide what information they would like; telephone numbers, library indexing, chemical formulas, personal aide-mémoires, train timetables, can be accessed and displayed quite as readily as the more normal range of management information.

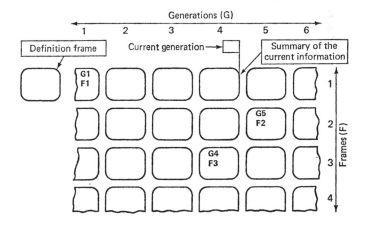

The matrix as shown in the illustration is arranged in columns called 'generations', each column being made up of a number of frames. Thus each frame has a unique generation and frame number. Frequently within the Management Terminal System the convention has been adopted of using the generations to represent time. Thus, if weekly information is being displayed, each generation would represent a particular week. Also within the Management Terminal System the first frame within any generation is frequently used to contain a summary of the information, whilst the other frames give a more detailed breakdown. However, it is important to emphasize that these are only conventions adopted within this particular application, and do not represent technical restrictions imposed by the design of the system.

One particular generation is flagged as the 'current' generation. On inputting the question number of the subject he wishes to interrogate, the user gains access to the first frame in the current generation. This is particularly significant when the generations are being used to record time. What the users require is to access the most up-to-date summary information, before deciding whether to seek more detail by searching down a generation, or to make comparisons in time by searching across a generation.

In addition to the matrix of frames each question number is supported by a definition frame. The important part this plays is described later.

Once the user has gained access to the first frame of the current generation, he can move freely within the matrix by using the action instructions explained below.

Explanatory note 3

Most of the action instructions are self-explanatory, as they represent simple one-way movements; more involved ones are explained below.

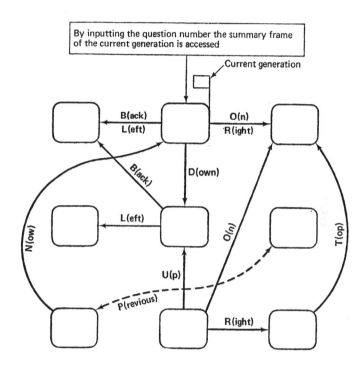

O(n) and B(ack) always access the first frame of the subsequent or preceding generation, whereas R(ight) and L(eft) access a frame of the subsequent or preceding generations bearing the same frame number as the one currently being accessed.

T(op) will access the first frame of the generation currently being accessed, whereas N(ow) will always access the first frame of the current generation, regardless of the frame currently being accessed. P(revious) is a particularly useful facility when a user wishes to compare two sets of figures. By inputting P he can recall the frame he has just left; thus he can see-saw between the two frames by continuing to input P. Every frame has a unique identity made up from the question number, the generation number and the frame number. If he wishes to do so, and if he knows these numbers, the user can access an individual frame by inputting its identity.

125

Step 5

The index of questions on External Data gave Share Price as question 33.

Share Price is an example of a continually changing piece of information; there are occasions when it attracts considerable interest, and therefore the information is updated three times each day.

The frequency with which each question is updated is dictated by the nature of the information contained therein. Operations at senior level rarely require information to be frequently updated. More usually information is presented on a weekly or four-monthly basis. This is certainly not a real-time on-line information retrieval system!

Because it would be both unnecessary and wasteful to store for comparative purposes details of the Share Price every time it is updated, the matrix has been designed to record weekly information over a span of up to twenty-five four-week periods. Each generation represents a four-week period and each frame presents the Share Price at close of trading on the Wednesday of one week during the four. The current generation is used to display 'today's' price, thus this is the frame accessed on inputting question 33. This arrangement is illustrated below.

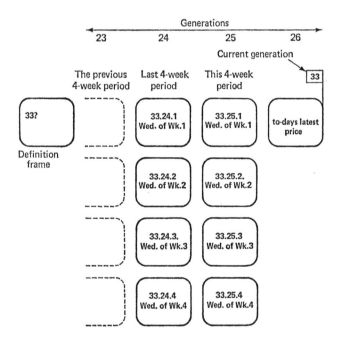

Step 6

This is an example of the information that was contained in the current generation of question 33 at noon on 20 August 1971.

33.26.1			FINANCIAL NEWS
	FINANCIAL NEWS SUMMARY		
	SHARE PRICES		
	TODAY	1971	
	20.8.71	HIGH	LOW
	P	P	P
IC(H)	108	175	103
GEC	157	160	90
PLESSEY	127	154	100

F.T. INDEX ROSE 4·0 TO 409·1 AT NOON AUGUST 20TH, 71

BANK RATE 6% CHANGED APRIL 1ST, 1971

PRICES AT: NOON AUGUST 20TH, 1971

B= AUGUST 11TH, 1971

By locating a particular subject within a particular chapter, and accessing that subject through its question number, the user has opened up for himself the matrix of information frames relevant to that subject. Starting with the information in the current generation he can search through the matrix, moving freely forward, backward and in depth, to provide himself with the information he is seeking.

However, even after this search, his quest for information may remain unsatisfied; it is in these circumstances that he makes use of the 'definition frame'. In order to access the definition frame the user once again inputs the question number; but this time he follows it with a question mark, thus . . . 33?

Step 7

The definition frame serves three distinct functions. The first function is to describe briefly the nature of the information provided in the matrix, and to define any special terms that are used. The second function is to list the question number of any related questions; this is an extraction from the question index but may list questions from more than one chapter. The third function is perhaps the most important, as it takes the user outside the system by giving him the name and telephone number of the executive whose responsibilities are reflected in the question. The executive to whom the user is referred may also be a user of the system and may have available to him the information the first user requires. If he wishes to do so he can instruct the system to make his question available to the first user, who is then able to access it through his own terminal. Alternatively, he can, of course, provide the answer verbally or in writing, supported by whatever explanation he thinks necessary.

The significance of involving these responsible executives in the supply of information is discussed more fully elsewhere in this chapter.

The following example, in which all the elements described are present, is of the definition frame for question 33.

33?	FINANCIAL NEWS
THIS QUESTION:	RELEVANT QUESTION:
SHARE PRICES FOR IC(H)	34 UK ELECTRONIC INDUST.
GEC, PLESSEY	PUBLISHED ACCOUNTS
BANK RATE AND F.T. INDEX	35 USA AND EUROPEAN
	ELEC. IND. PUBL'D ACCOUNTS
HISTORIC INFORMATION ON	39 ELECTRONIC EQUIP. MKT.
A WEEKLY BASIS	49 COMPETITIVE INFORMTN.
	100 SUMMARY OF SHARE PRICES
TYPE N FOR TODAY'S PRICES	101 AV. SHARE PRICE 70/71
	102 SHARE STRENGTH 70/71
	103 AV. SHARE PRICE 69/70
	104 SHARE STRENGTH 69/70
	105 DAILY SHARES AT NOON

UPDATED: DAILY AT 10·00/NOON/CLOSE
SOURCE: SHARE REGISTRAR
      FOR FURTHER INFORMATION CONTACT:
    J. SMITH, SHARE REGISTRAR, HEAD OFFICE,
        EXTN. 5234

Step 8

The various ways in which the system can be used have already been explained. Question 33, about the Share Price, presented a good example of a matrix of information which the user entered through a current generation frame, giving the most up-to-date summary of the information.

Question 45, illustrated below, shows a different category of information by presenting a straight list of the staff of the Department of Trade and Industry. In this case the O(n) and B(ack) facilities are not used, and the list continues, using the D(own) facility until it is completed.

45.1.1   DEPARTMENT OF TRADE AND INDUSTRY
HEADQUARTERS, 1, VICTORIA STREET, S.W.1.
01-222-7877

SECRETARY OF STATE	JOHN DAVIES, MBE
MINISTER FOR TRADE	MICHAEL NOBLE
MINISTER FOR INDUSTRY	SIR JOHN EDEN, BT
MINISTER FOR AEROSPACE	FREDERICK CORFIELD
PARL. UNDER SEC. TRADE	ANTHONY GRANT
PARL. UNDER SEC. INDUSTRY	NICHOLAS RIDLEY
PERMANENT SECRETARY	SIR ANTHONY PART, KCB, MBE
2ND PERM. SEC. TRADE	SIR MAX BROWN, KCB, CMG
2ND PERM. SEC. INDUSTRY	R. B. MARSHALL, CB, MBE
DEPUTY SECRETARY	W. HUGHES, CB
CHIEF SCIENTIST	DR. I. MADDOCK, CB, OBE, FRS
HEAD OF RESEARCH	DR. E. LEE
INDUSTRIAL ADVISORS	D. W. HARDY
	A. C. BUCK
	O. J. LISTON
	B. R. AITKEN

D(OWN)=CONTINUED

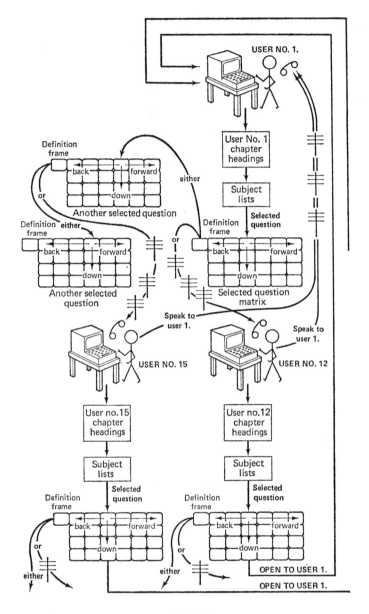

Fig. 6.4

Summary

The following illustration summarizes the range of searching facilities available to a user of the Management Terminal System. The flexibility of the system and the ease with which information can be made available and transmitted alleviate the technical problems associated with supplying management information. The essential problem of 'What information?' remains. This is an intellectual problem that requires men to think about the nature of their job, rather than about the technical problems of obtaining information to help them think about the nature of their job!

The ICL Management Terminal System was studied as part of a research project being undertaken by the Department of Ergonomics and Cybernetics at the University of Technology of Loughborough into man-computer interaction, especially at higher levels such as managerial decision-making.

With their permission I am reproducing the conclusions that they reached and some of their findings.

CONCLUSIONS[1]

Top managers making regular use of visual display units remain very few in number. The cost of developing these systems and the problem of providing a useful and easy-to-use service to busy managers are currently preventing their widespread implementation. Notwithstanding the obvious commercial advantage to ICL of leading the field in the use of its own products, the Management Terminal System survives because it has solved the problem of being useful and easy to use. It is to the credit of system designers that it requires the very minimum of that scarce management commodity, time.

The existing system, while useful, provides no service that could not be provided by other, less expensive means. Before the unique properties of the interactive visual display units are used to full benefit, the scope and sophistication of the systems must be increased. Users have many ideas for the development of the system, all of which will increase its complexity. This means that the design problem, of increasing the service of the system while retaining its ease of use, will become progressively more difficult.

[1] Extracts from the HUSAT no. 17 reproduced with the permission of Mr K. Eason and Professor B. Shakel of the Department of Ergonomics and Cybernetics of the University of Technology, Loughborough, and of Mr Alan F. Edwards, Finance Director, ICL.

131

FINDINGS: ABSTRACT OF USER COMMENTS

Factors affecting their satisfaction with the system

The system provided accurate information

No major gaps in the information

The users found the 5–10-second response time satisfactory, the occasional 20 seconds were frustrating

A more expensive system merely to improve response time not justified

Standard of information presentation excellent

Screen too small but they adapted to its limitations[1]

Introduction of graphical facilities a priority

They sometimes lost their way and went back to the beginning

They unanimously praised the simplicity of instructions and procedures

They relied too heavily upon the list of available questions

All were strongly in favour of the security codes

The principle of matching information access to the hierarchical distribution of responsibilities is supported

The positions of the terminal in the office posed no problems as it is mobile

No users used the terminals in meetings

Although no users found it difficult to work without the system, they did find it irritating and annoying

They did not need to know any more about the system

Main uses mentioned

Easy-to-use filing cabinet

Made information available without having to seek the information from a colleague

Demonstrates ICL products to potential customers; important but did not justify the system

Catalytic effect in making directors think about the nature of their business

Encouraged staff to develop techniques of future commercial value

Great potential for the future

---

[1] A visual display unit with a large screen is being introduced into the system shortly.

132

Effects upon their method of working

Encouraged them to develop new ideas or methods

Gave them greater insight into the nature of information and its function

Eased the work load of gathering information from various sources

Changed the extent and nature of their communication with others

Led to more effective communication

Discussion points made in the report

The M.T.S. is one of the very few working systems located

Those who have tried such systems have usually failed

The M.T.S. is both relevant and easy to use

That it remains in use over a year after implementation is a matter for congratulation

It is very easy to learn and requires the minimum of effort to use

Conclusion

This book set out to restore a balance. Its aim was to give those people with little technical background enough confidence to be able to direct technical activity so that it can become subservient to their needs. No man can know and understand all things: the technical man must know when he should call for assistance from the world around him to help him use his technology in a practical way, and the non-technical man needs to know when he should call for assistance from the technical man. The man in the street needs to know when he should seek help from a doctor. The doctor seeks help from a bank manager; the bank manager seeks help from an architect; the architect seeks help from a builder. Lin Yutang wrote in *The Importance of Living*:

'And as you take a stroll through the city, you see that back of the main avenue with beauty parlours and flower shops and shipping firms is another street with drug stores, grocery stores, hardware shops, barber shops, laundries, cheap eating places, news-stands. You wander along for an hour, and if it is a big city, you are still there; you see only more streets, more drug stores, grocery stores, hardware shops, barber shops, laundries, cheap eating places and news-stands. How do these people make their living? And why do they come here? Very simple. The laundrymen wash the clothes of the barbers and restaurant workers, the restaurant workers wait upon the laundrymen and barbers while they eat, and the barbers cut the hair of the laundrymen and waiters.'

Human activity requires the maintaining of a balance between all the activities, emotions and learning of mankind. New things that emerge can upset this balance, especially if, like computers, they are powerful and difficult to comprehend.

134

This book has attempted to restore the balance not by teaching the technology, but by exploring some of the problems which face organizations, and by showing how computers can help to solve those problems. One does not need to be a motor mechanic to drive a motor-car, an electronic engineer to watch a television programme, a chemist to take an aspirin. One needs sufficient confidence in what these things can do, so that in relevant situations one can use them.

Because of their newness, their complexity and the rate of technological development, computers dominate their surroundings. By placing them in the historical context of other new things, and in the human context of man's reaction to change, some of the awe disappears and we can bridge the gulf between people and the computer.

I chose as the theme for this book the use of computers in managing organizations. However, it soon became apparent that the real problem lay in understanding the organization, and with the reaction of people to situations. With this as a starting point it was much easier to see the ways in which the computer could serve the organization. A number of loosely defined, quasi-technical terms have been generated by the computer industry; data base and management information systems are two which have been examined closely in this book to show how little they have to do with computers, and what a lot they have to do with understanding the nature of the organization.

This book has explored some of the opportunities which the power of computing provides to those concerned with managing situations and taking significant decisions. The common thread throughout, however, has been the people: the people who take the decisions, the people who are responsible for the data and the information, the people who devise computing systems.

The way in which the data is controlled, the way in which the models are constructed, the way in which information is presented, are all reflections of the policy of the organization.

It is not sufficient within an organization to have a policy for the supply of computing resources; this policy needs to go hand in glove with a data policy, an information policy, and a policy for the selection and progressing of computer applications. One of the most urgent tasks facing many organizations is the need to develop these policies.

Computing power—and the things that can be done with it—is very new; it is powerful, it is expensive, and it is remorseless. It responds blindly and inevitably to the instructions it receives. Give it a wrong instruction, point a system in the wrong direction, and the results are wasteful, expensive and sometimes catastrophic!

135

The initiative in exploiting the power of computers, in formulating the necessary policies within an organization, must come from its managers. It cannot be delegated to the technical management, to the data-progressing staff.

Given these policies, the organization can expect increasing support for its plans, decisions and operations using managers and computers to concentrate separately on doing the things they can do best.